CARDIFF
Rebirth of a Capital

Cardiff Council in conjunction with
Cardiff University and the People of Cardiff

Edited by Mike Ungersma
Original Photography by David Hurn
Foreword by Dame Shirley Bassey

CARDIFF
CAERDYDD

CONTENTS

CARDIFF
CAERDYDD

Publisher - Cardiff Council
Editor - Mike Ungersma
Photographer - David Hurn
Designer - Jason Hennessy

Additional photography by Charles &
Patricia Aithie / ffotograff

All images © photographers

A catalogue record for the book is
available from the British Library

ISBN 0 902466 22 4

Printed in UK by Butler & Tanner

FOREWORD
by Dame Shirley Bassey

"Thank You for the Years was the album I made in 2003 to mark my 50th year in show business. More than 60 albums! Can you believe it? A kid from the Cardiff Docks, and all she ever wanted to do was sing? And it's just as hard to believe the changes I've seen in Cardiff. It too has an anniversary to celebrate – 50 years as the capital of Wales. And another one I certainly don't remember! It was 100 years ago that it officially became a city.

For me, my latest album is a way of saying "Thanks." And that's important, because wherever singing has taken me over the years, it's the tens of thousands of fans who believed in me who made it happen, starting with my mates at the enamelware factory in Splott where I used to pack pots in brown paper. They were the first to encourage me to sing at the club dances. It was the first time I wore high heels and lipstick! I was 15 then, had just left school and dreamed of being everything from an air hostess to a model.

I left Cardiff two years later and the Cardiff of today is as different as I am a person, as all of us are. They've tamed the tiger in my Tiger Bay! Is it better now than it was then? That's a question I'm often asked. It's moved on as we have. And no one would have it any other way. I'm a romantic – just listen to my songs! – but I'm also realistic. The Tiger Bay I left as a girl, hoping to make it big in the big, wide world, had to change. Few of us raised in those friendly old neighbourhoods would recognise them today. Who would know the street or house they were born in all these years later? But look at them now. Better? More like the Ritz compared to the streets I knew. It's easy to forget that times were tough then. Mum had seven mouths to feed, and we weren't any different from neighbours and friends.

I grew up and Cardiff grew up too. Who would have ever thought it?

Cardiff changed because it had to change with the world around it, and a lot of thinking and imagination has gone into planning how best to get that change right. You only have to look around you to see it. When I went to London for an audition in 1953, no one there had ever heard of Cardiff. For a long, long time after that, as I toured the world, I had to point to a map to show people my hometown and Wales. No more. That is how Cardiff and Wales has changed – now we're on everyone's map! I had dreams when I was young, and mine came true. And now they are coming true for Cardiff too.

As they say, the rest is history.

Happy Birthday, Cardiff! And *Thank You for the Years."*

"Thank You for the Years"

INTRODUCTION by Mike Ungersma

Cab drivers are an icon of the cities they serve. In New York, their ill-tempered response to anything, including a mere "hello," is notorious. On the other hand, London cabbies are brash, talk non-stop, and will offer an opinion on anything from controversial Mayor Ken Livingstone to the much maligned Millennium Dome – even if you haven't asked. But arrive at Cardiff Central train station and the cabbie who greets you is more apt to boast of the city's civic centre or the redevelopment of its waterfront, the once grim 'Tiger Bay.'

Being an American meant that for the first few years that I lived in the Welsh capital, taking a cab also meant having the same conversation with the driver. "Here's a tourist," they thought, and like cabbies everywhere, they specialise in haranguing foreigners. Now most of them know me, and the situation is reversed: I am telling them about their city. The reason? Journalistic curiosity more than anything else. You see, I work in their magnificent 'Civic Centre', the product of a remarkable burst of 19th Century citizen enthusiasm that helped transform Cardiff from an insignificant market town into one of the UK's most resplendent Victorian cities. It happened, and indeed was made possible, because at that time Cardiff was the world's largest coal exporter. So important was it as a port that it was chosen by Captain Robert Falcon Scott when he left on his ill-fated voyage to the South Pole in 1910.

Where I teach at Cardiff University overlooks Cathays Park, the Civic Centre referred to by cabbies. When I joined the University 15 years ago, I asked colleagues, 'Who built this complex?' 'Who was responsible for this enormous and impressive square of public buildings?' Each is built of softly radiant Portland stone, surely one of the most exquisite building materials ever provided by nature. Their answers were pretty vague, and that's why I decided to find out. You see, I arrived in Cardiff when it was about to undertake a second mammoth project – the restoration and redevelopment of 2,700 acres of derelict docklands, the 'Tiger Bay' of legend and song. Then it was in ruin, a virtual bombsite. Cardiff had made a fundamental mistake in the 19th and early 20th Centuries. It relied on a single product for its prosperity – the coal which lay in incalculable abundance beneath the hills of the South Wales Valleys above the city. The coal didn't run out. As a matter of fact, there are still vast reserves of it left in Wales and elsewhere in Great Britain. It was replaced by oil. And the replacement was quick, dramatic and disastrous. What was left in the way of the 'good old times,' a period of unparalleled prosperity, was finished off by the Great Depression and the wrenching experience of the Second World War.

By the 1950s, Cardiff was back where it had been a century before; insignificant and unimportant. The Civic Centre was there, but little else. A triple blow of the dethronement of 'King Coal,' the depression and the war had dealt it a knockout punch. This was a city that was going nowhere.

Then something happened, and this is the tricky part. Somehow, a handful of visionaries, men and women who insisted on looking to the future and not the once-glorious past, began to agitate for action. One was an academic, a city planner called George Yeomans. In a 1968 article in the Western Mail it was Yeomans who first suggested the redevelopment of the vast and virtually abandoned docks area. Whether it was Yeomans' foresight that galvanized others to action is something we will never know, but action began and by the early 1980s, an ambitious plan was underway. There were sceptics as there always are in such undertakings, but unlike its curiously negative attitude toward the Civic Centre of more than a century earlier, this time the Western Mail and its sister paper, the South Wales Echo, stood behind the project and promoted its virtues tirelessly.

The Bay endeavour, spearheaded by a unique (for the UK) public and private partnership inspired by the American city of Baltimore, was underway. It would take the better part of two decades, and even today is not finished. But the foundation and much of the structures – new offices, restaurants, cinemas, homes, apartments, light industry, and above all, the barrage halting for all time the tides of the River Taff – are in place. The city centre, already redeveloped into one of the most attractive and stunning

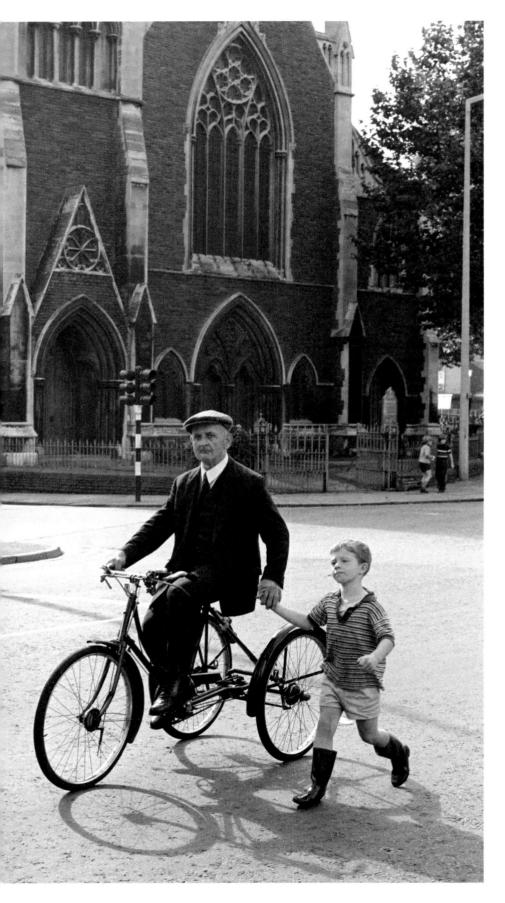

shopping areas in the UK, is now re-connected with its equally stunning waterfront, a unification that has made Cardiff one of Europe's most appealing and livable communities.

What took place here, and what continues to take place, is a momentum and drive that is almost palpable, even spiritual – you can feel the dynamism. The negative side of a once bleak ledger of decline has been forever reversed. The Cardiff Bay re-development, St. David's Shopping Centre and its world-class auditorium St David's Hall, a new rugby stadium so large even astronauts must be able to see it, the designation of Cardiff as the capital of Wales, and the siting in the city of the new Welsh Assembly – all add up to a truly remarkable transformation by a people who once appeared defeated; a people who had once carried an unbearable burden of decline.

The story of how this was achieved deserves telling, and it is precisely the task this book addresses. It does so on a particularly notable occasion, 2005 – Cardiff's 50th anniversary as the capital of Wales, and the city's 100th birthday. Cardiff has had its share of books looking at its past. This one chronicles its recent and remarkable rise to become "the youngest capital in Europe," and very much looks forward to its future.

That Cardiff's 'tomorrow' is about as positive, promising and auspicious as any city could hope for. In my research, work that led me to write a book about the city that unashamedly celebrates the achievements of its people and all of the Welsh, I open with a quotation from the Welsh-born scholar Raymond Williams. While he wasn't talking about Cardiff, he easily could have been when he remarked: "This is what men have achieved – are not all things then possible?"

Mike Ungersma
Cardiff University

The Great Transformation
Chapter 1

Adapted from text by

Gillian Bristow & Kevin Morgan

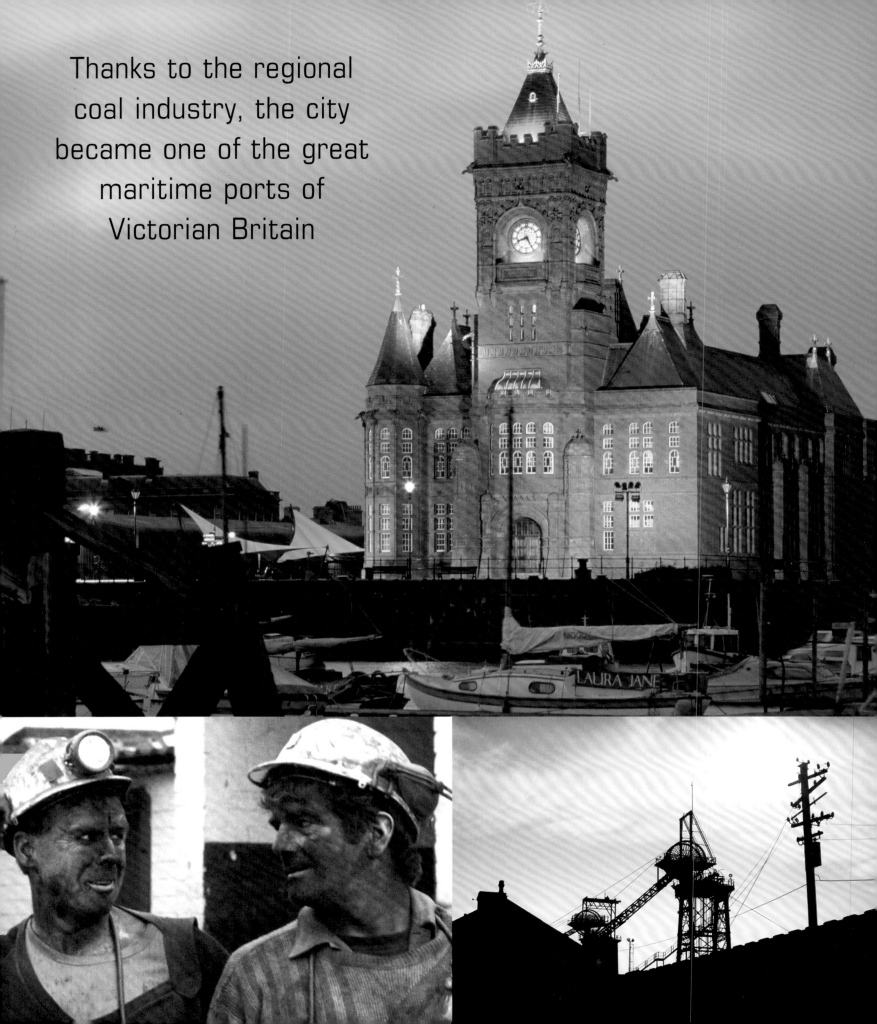

Thanks to the regional coal industry, the city became one of the great maritime ports of Victorian Britain

ew British cities have undergone more dramatic economic change than Cardiff during the 20th Century. Thanks to the regional coal industry, the city became one of the great maritime ports of Victorian Britain. By the late 19th Century the local docks were handling a greater tonnage of goods per acre than any other port in the country, and by the early 20th Century it became the biggest coal exporting port in the world. Remarkably, this was the city where the world's first £1 million cheque was signed. But if the growth of the coal industry elevated Cardiff into a major city, its decline could very easily have been the kiss of death for the young coal metropolis.

A 'coal rush' now took place in the valleys of the south. Above all, the two Rhonddas became the 'Black Klondyke.' In 1850 trout still leapt in the clear waters that ran through the weep woodlands of Llwynypia – the Magpie's Grove. Fifty years later there wasn't a trout or magpie in the whole deep valley. Long lines of terraced houses choked the lower slopes. The wheels turned day and night over mine shafts dropping their cages over a thousand feet to the lucrative Rhondda No. 3 seam. The endless trains of coal trucks rattled down to the docks at Cardiff and Barry, where ships of the world crowded the roads to wait their turn at the coal hoists. This was the real Rape of the Fair Country.

'WALES: A HISTORY'
WYNFORD VAUGHAN-THOMAS
(MICHAEL JOSEPH, 1985)

That it managed to survive the disastrous decline of the coal trade, and reinvent itself as a post-industrial capital city where service sector jobs now dominate, says something about the vitality of the city and its people. And, as importantly, it also says something about the re-birth of Wales as a nation. Indeed, the growth of Cardiff owes much to the public sector functions which attended the devolution of power, a process which culminated in the creation of the National Assembly in 1999. It is this interplay between the city and the nation that helps us to understand how Cardiff managed to emerge from the ashes of a coal metropolis to become a city worthy of a role on the world stage.

Although we speak of Cardiff as a post-industrial city today, it's worth asking whether it was ever a real 'industrial city' in the strictest sense of the term. Thirty years ago, when the manufacturing industry accounted for more than a third of total employment in the UK, and nearly a third of all jobs in Wales, it accounted for only one in five jobs in Cardiff. And by 2001, the manufacturing sector in Cardiff had shrunk to such an extent that it employed a mere nine per cent of the urban workforce, compared to more than 17 per cent in Wales and 14 per cent in the UK.

If we look at long-term employment, two key trends stand out apart from the de-industrialisation itself. Over the period as a whole the single most dramatic change was the rapid growth of banking, finance and insurance. In 1974, only a tiny fraction of people – seven per cent – worked in these 'white collar' occupations. By the turn of the century it had leapt to one in five. The other key trend has been the steady, if less dramatic, growth of jobs in Cardiff's public administration, health and education institutions, far and away the most important employment sector in terms of the biggest employer.

These changes in employment also meant a shift in what people earned. In that earlier period – 1974 – earnings for male and female employees were marginally higher in Cardiff than in the UK as a whole. By 2001 average earnings for both men and women lagged way behind their UK counterparts.

There was also another fundamental change during that period – an increase in the female workforce. Although this process occurred throughout the country, it was more pronounced in Cardiff with the number of women at work increasing from four out of every ten workers to over half by 2001.

Out went the factories – as few as they may have been – and in came the 'service' industry, which today accounts for a staggering 90 percent of all employment in Cardiff, a level that is well above that of other cities in the UK. Since the 1980s Cardiff has become a true 'post-industrial' city characterised by a vibrant shopping centre and a growing leisure, tourism, restaurant and hotel sector. Indeed, almost a quarter of the city's workforce is now employed in distribution, hotels and restaurants – a proportion higher than many larger cities such as Bristol, Liverpool, Manchester and Edinburgh. Since the late 1990s, leisure complexes have been developed in and around Cardiff Bay – look at Atlantic Wharf and Mermaid Quay – as well as in the city centre, much of it focused on the Millennium Stadium and Mary Anne Street south of the city centre.

This growth was hugely fed by the spending of the city's expanding student population. Cardiff has three higher education institutions – Cardiff University, the University of Wales Institute Cardiff (UWIC) and the Welsh College of Music and Drama. The huge economic and cultural contribution made by these institutions includes their role as major employers in Cardiff and the market created by the spending of tens of thousands of students.

Cardiff University is one of Britain's leading teaching and research universities with an international reputation which attracts staff and students from around the world. The merger in 2004 of the University and the College of Medicine has created a larger and more dynamic university with increased capabilities and capacities based on unification and associated additional strategic investment. This has created a world-class, competitive university and an education powerhouse able to make even stronger contributions to the intellectual, economic, health and social well-being of Wales.

Staging of international events in the city plays an important role in stimulating growth in the service industries in Cardiff. Cardiff successfully hosted a major European Summit in 1998, and the Millennium Stadium played host to the Rugby World Cup in 1999 as well as the final of football's premier domestic tournament, the FA Cup.

As a result, Cardiff is now a major attraction for international visitors. Just as crucial is the fact Cardiff is the largest retail centre in Wales – even larger than its nearest English competitor, Bristol. With its wide range and variety of department, specialist and variety stores – many of them connected by the quaint and world famous Victorian arcades – Cardiff is one of the most popular shopping destinations in the entire country.

The story of Cardiff's service economy has been strongly shaped by the public sector where three out of 10 Cardiff residents work. This is considerably higher than the national average, and higher than cities such as Edinburgh, Bristol and Manchester. The three biggest employers in Cardiff are all within the public sector, namely Cardiff Council, Cardiff and Vale NHS Trust and

Cardiff University. Indeed, Cardiff Council is the biggest single employer in Wales, with over 18,000 employees in over 200 locations across the city. And it is a big 'business' by any measure, with an annual turnover of two-thirds of a billion pounds, and spending £13 million per week on a wide range of services.

As well as its direct contribution to the local economy, the public sector played a significant if indirect role in shaping Cardiff's transition from a manufacturing to a service-based economy. The dramatic economic transformation of the city since the '70s reflects the strong support given by the Council to leisure and retail-linked property development. For example, the opening of County Hall in 1988 acted as a powerful catalyst for the subsequent residential and leisure development in Atlantic Wharf. Similarly, Council support was important in facilitating the provision of key employment sites, office space and premises.

> My worst nightmare is Wales as a nation of wine waiters and museum attendants.
>
> **GWYN A. WILLIAMS**
> WHEN WAS WALES? (PENGUIN BOOKS, 1985)

The regeneration of Cardiff Bay now attracts office, retail, leisure and residential development. By the beginning of 1998, development activity added a staggering 114,000 square metres of office space to the city's 'stock'. This was a direct result of the ballooning in demand for major office space, prompted by the availability of financial incentives to encourage companies and organisations to move to certain key locations and the increase in refurbished offices. Cardiff also has a generous share of suburban retailing, including a full range Marks & Spencer five miles from the city centre at Culverhouse Cross, and the Cardiff Bay Retail Park, which is home to one of the largest Ikea stores in the UK.

Cardiff has become particularly successful in recent years in attracting major financial and business service providers. It is the main financial and business service

centre in Wales, and continues to grow in importance, accounting for more than one fifth of Cardiff's total workforce.

> Cardiff is now a financial centre with bank, insurance companies, mortgage lender and ancillary and support companies providing substantial employment opportunities. These activities have probably reached a critical mass and with the support of excellent educational facilities, Cardiff should continue to attract employers in these key areas of a modern economy.
>
> **SIR DONALD WALTERS**
> VICE CHAIRMAN, INSTITUTE OF WELSH AFFAIRS,
> AND FORMER MANAGING DIRECTOR,
> THE HODGE GROUP

The sector grew steadily in recent years, with a particularly rapid spurt in the 1980s and 1990s. During this period the city benefited from the westward expansion of development along the M4 corridor, as companies moved their routine 'back-office' operations such as data processing and call centres from the congested southeast of England. This turned out to be a hugely successful strategy for attracting major inward investment.

Financial services employment continued to grow in Cardiff during the 1990s but at a much slower rate. Substantial investments were made by insurance firms such as Admiral, NCM Credit and AXA. This was accompanied by a growth in real estate around the burgeoning Cardiff Bay development. Cardiff did, however, suffer from banking re-organisation in the 1990s and has only a few foreign banks and headquarters or regional offices.

> With a 1st or 2nd class degree I can be looking at any engineering or computing management job - after a few years of job experience. I have a job lined up for when I graduate, relocating to Cardiff to work for BT in their software house.
>
> **DAVID OSBORN**
> STUDENT,
> LEICESTER UNIVERSITY

With a 1st or 2nd class degree I can be looking at any engineering or computing management job

David Osborn,
Student, Leicester University

Employment continues to increase in direct telebanking and insurance, and more recently in the expansion of telephone call centres and wider customer contact centres. Indeed, Cardiff has become one of the most significant clusters of call and contact centre activity in the whole of the UK. The attraction of call centres has been one of the most successful strands of the Council's inward investment strategy, and has been given added impetus through the activities of the All Wales Call Centre Forum - a partnership of relevant agencies. A number of major companies have established large call centres in Cardiff. These include Legal and General, Zurich, Bank One International, the Inland Revenue, AA Insurance and 118UK.

Cardiff represents an attractive location for call centres and newer contact centres, including those now concentrating on providing web-enabled services. These include ample and diverse office space, and office rental costs which are as much as a third below the UK average, and significantly lower than competitor locations such as Bristol, Swindon and Reading. Cardiff also benefits from access to a large pool of flexible and low-cost workers, and increasingly, graduates. Call centre operators in and around Cardiff are able to find skilled and motivated workers from an area that includes the industrial south Wales valleys where earnings were always lower. The city also enjoys good road and rail links, conveniently situated on the M4. This means eight out of ten people in the UK can reach Cardiff in four hours. Excellent high speed rail services and the six international airports within easy reach give rapid access to all major UK and European cities. Cardiff also benefits from a sophisticated and low-cost telecommunications infrastructure.

The call centre industry faces some important challenges ahead, not least of which is the growing threat of employment shifting abroad. Improving the quality of employment in the sector in Cardiff is also a key challenge. A priority for the future must be to attract higher value added activities to the city. Whilst labour turnover in call and contact centres in Cardiff is considerably lower than in many other parts of the UK, the retention of good quality staff through training, the provision of a good working environment and appropriate salaries will clearly become more important issues in the future.

> Welsh call centres must be very competent in managing and retaining people as their attrition figures are the best in the British Isles, with salaries now on a par with the rest of the UK. Supervisory management appears to be particularly competent in Wales.
>
> **MICHAEL ALLEN**
> MANAGING DIRECTOR,
> MITIAL RESEARCH INTERNATIONAL

Given the trend towards de-industrialisation in the UK, Cardiff has overcome the downward slide. It retains a range of national and international manufacturing companies like NEG, Panasonic, IQE, AB Automotive Electronics, ATL Telecom and Allied Steel and Wire (ASW), now owned by the Spanish company Celsa. Though small, this manufacturing sector is vital in adding diversity to the service economy, providing a range of skilled and semi-skilled employment opportunities in an otherwise post-industrial city. The stories of ASW and Panasonic are particularly notable because they highlight the national and international pressures that combine to make life so difficult for the manufacturing sector in the UK.

Before it was acquired by Celsa in 2002, ASW was one of the largest manufacturing concerns in Cardiff, with 3,500 employees at its peak. Formed in 1981 as a joint venture between GKN and British Steel, ASW signalled a new phase in a steel-making tradition in Cardiff that stretched back to the 1890s and whose origins lay in the city's close links with the Dowlais works in Merthyr and the Guest family.

Excellent high speed rail services and the six international airports within easy reach give rapid access to all major UK and European cities

Although wage levels in Cardiff and Wales are lower than much of the UK, they are high in relation to some new competing countries

Following a management buy-out in 1987 the prospects for ASW looked bright at first because it was supplying special steel products for the construction industry. But a series of adverse factors – in particular a downturn in the construction industry, an ill-fated acquisition of a French steel company and an increasingly uncompetitive exchange rate - forced ASW into mounting debt and eventual receivership in July 2002, with the tragic loss of 1000 well-paid jobs.

If ASW highlights the problem of manufacturing in the context of an overvalued exchange rate, Panasonic highlights the dilemma of being a manufacturer of price sensitive consumer electronics products. Panasonic opened its factory in Pentwyn in the 1970s when a number of Japanese consumer electronics firms decided to follow the example of Sony, which opened its main European TV plant in Bridgend in 1974.

> It's clear we have to move up the value chain as companies like Sony and Sharp migrate to countries with low labour costs.
>
> **RHODRI MORGAN**
> FIRST MINISTER OF THE NATIONAL ASSEMBLY

The Japanese plants were relatively secure sources of semi-skilled employment until recently, when consumer electronic prices began to fall in response to more intense competition from low cost countries in Eastern Europe and China.

Although wage levels in Cardiff and Wales are lower than much of the UK, they are high in relation to some new competing countries. The result is Japanese consumer electronic firms reducing their profiles in Wales in one of two ways: either through closing their plants – which Hitachi did at Hirwaun – or relocating basic production to one of the lower cost countries, precisely the move Panasonic made in transferring some product lines from Cardiff to the Czech Republic.

Although Wales was relatively successful for a time as a niche location for low cost, semi-skilled production, this strategy has been overtaken by lower cost countries, many now members of the European Union. This means that internationally mobile firms like Panasonic need to be persuaded its Cardiff plant is capable of making more sophisticated products – products that are less price sensitive. If Cardiff is to maintain a viable manufacturing sector, as it

must if it is to offer a diversity of employment, its manufacturing firms have to become more specialised and more 'knowledge intensive' in their operations.

> The managerial, financial, research and development, engineering, technical and marketing skills that drive the modern economy have remained firmly rooted outside Wales.
>
> **JOHN BALL**
> SWANSEA BUSINESS SCHOOL

One way to foster this value-adding process is to promote better technology transfer partnerships between industry and the universities in Wales. The city is fortunate in having a strong academic research base in this sector in the form of the Manufacturing Engineering Centre at Cardiff

become as significant a development as the opening of the M4 30 years ago. This centre provides an ultra-secure data storage facility to run business internet and e-commerce facilities and should provide an important platform for future IT business development.

Cardiff has ambitions to become a knowledge-based economy, or one dominated by high technology industries

University and the National Centre for Product Design and Development Research at UWIC, both recognised as Centres of Excellence.

In addition to these initatives, the Cardiff Business Technology Centre which is jointly funded by the Council and the European Regional Development Fund, provides support and assistance to facilitate the growth of new technology businesses and science based enterprise in the city.

In common with many other European and British cities, Cardiff has ambitions to become a knowledge-based economy, or one dominated by high technology industries and services such as telecommunications, computer and information equipment and services. Much progress has been made towards ensuring that Cardiff has the fibre optic connections and other key IT infrastructure to help achieve this. Indeed, Cardiff benefits from nearly total broadband coverage. And, in partnership with BT and Cardiff University's e-Commerce Innovation Centre, the Council is working to promote the use of broadband technology amongst local businesses. It has an innovative wireless internet or wi-fi programme which provides wireless broadband coverage throughout the city centre and in Cardiff Bay. The BT Ignite Data Centre in Cardiff Bay also represents an important development that may

When I proposed in the mid-'60s that the number of university students should be planned to treble to 15,000 by the year 2000, it was thought to be unrealistic. Today, those attending Cardiff University and the University of Wales Institute total 30,000 – 10 per cent of Cardiff 's population.

EWART PARKINSON
FORMER CITY PLANNING OFFICER
OF CARDIFF

Cardiff's ambition to become a knowledge-based economy has also thrown the spotlight on the role played by the city's higher education institutions as engines for economic growth and development. As well as their direct role as major employers and purchasers in the local economy, universities are increasingly an integral part of the city and regional network of public facilities. Why? Because they act as centres of attraction for individuals and enterprises, modifying the qualification structure of our workforce and improving virtually everyone's skills. Over 4,000 students graduate from these institutions in Cardiff each year - many stay here and contribute incalculably. Providing more high-quality jobs in future means even more will make this city their city.

Wales is now the largest broadcast centre outside of London, much of it clustered in and around Cardiff

Everyone recognises how film, TV and multimedia have expanded in Cardiff, indeed it was the fastest growing sector of all in the last decade. Employment shot upwards by more than 40 per cent, bringing the total number of jobs to 3,550, compared to 2,500 jobs in 1991. The traditional film and TV industry in Wales has generally been strong relative to the size of the Welsh economy, and Wales is now the largest broadcast centre outside London, much of it clustered in and around Cardiff. In addition to the major broadcasters of BBC Wales, S4C and HTV, and largely because of them, there is a vibrant independent TV production industry sector in Wales of over 600 companies employing an estimated 6,000 employees.

Many of these independent production companies – Green Bay, Fulmar, Derwen, Opus, Boomerang and Siriol Productions – are based in the capital for good reasons. When the Council surveyed them recently, they said that the reasons they make the city their headquarters include being closer to major clients like the BBC, ITV and S4C, that TV industry staff are already based in the city, the city's positive image and access to a larger pool of specialised labour.

The film, TV, radio and whole media sector is a key component of the wider 'cultural economy' or creative industry sector, and in 2000 Cardiff came ninth in the league table of UK cities in terms of its cultural economy, with 22,300 jobs, equivalent to more than 13 per cent of total employment in the city. At its heart in Cardiff, and the biggest single component of it by far, is BBC Wales. The direct and indirect employment effect of BBC Wales has driven the growth of the sector in recent years a kind of 'devolution dividend' in the sense that part of this growth was fuelled by new investment to cover the National Assembly for Wales.

BBC Wales has a double impact on film, TV and media in Wales: firstly through the direct effect of its own activities and, secondly, through the indirect effect of its purchasing of services and commissioning of programmes from the independents.

New opportunities could open up for independent companies following the regulatory changes introduced by the 2003 Communications Act. Like other broadcasters in the past, BBC Wales held back the growth of the independents by taking all the broadcast rights for itself when working with independents. Now that will change with the new law. Independent companies will retain their rights, an important change in a multi-channel TV environment and a potential source of extra revenue for small businesses who are often cash-strapped.

S4C has played a very important role in the Welsh economy since it was created in 1982, not least because nearly all of its programme budget of £73.5 million is spent in Wales. Both directly and indirectly this supports 2,000 jobs throughout Wales, the lion's share in Cardiff. In addition, S4C also acts as a lever for inward investment into Wales: every year S4C's role as broker of co-productions secures some £2 million of additional investment into Welsh productions. The Welsh animation industry owes its international renown and economic success to S4C's original investment. Importantly, S4C says it intends to continue that commitment.

If film and TV programme making is to have a viable future in Cardiff, then some of the pressing development issues – like the provision of training to a largely freelance workforce, access to finance for small businesses and commissions from other than BBC Wales and S4C – need to be resolved, and urgently.

Cardiff's very rapid rate of economic transformation in recent years has ensured that the city has enjoyed full employment. But there are still too many underprivileged neighbourhoods where deprivation remains a serious problem. The so-called 'southern arc' has an unemployment rate comparable with the worst in Wales. There are also parts that are too dependent on benefits such as income

Cardiff's very rapid rate of economic transformation in recent years has ensured the city enjoyed full employment

support. Many of those same areas have higher levels of ill health and child poverty. Encouraging wider participation of all Cardiff residents in the city's prosperity is a major challenge.

> It is generally noted that Wales has too many people signed off sick, suffers from a brain drain, depends too heavily on the public sector and manufacturing, and is beginning to lose activities such as TV-making and call centres, which saved its bacon after the swift and brutal decline of coal and steel.
>
> **"SAVING WALES"**
> MANAGEMENT TODAY (SEPTEMBER 2004)

However, there are no easy solutions to the problems of economic and social deprivation. The problems are too complex. The reasons are many, and include the concentration of new employment in certain parts of the city such as Pontprennau and Cardiff Bay, neither of which is easily accessible for people without a car. Then there are the difficulties in overcoming barriers to employment caused by ill health, disability, fear of crime and lack of childcare. All of this is the result of a complicated mix of economic, social and environmental factors which are often concentrated in certain areas and communities.

The challenge is made tougher by the fact that Cardiff's role as the capital of Wales is not sufficiently acknowledged at national level. There are additional costs in hosting major national events in the city, as well as extra pressure on services due to the daily inward migration of commuters. Yet these costs and pressures are not taken into account in the local government financial

settlement. Strikingly, 40p out of every £1 of rates paid by businesses in Cardiff goes to other Welsh local authorities.

Despite these constraints, positive steps are being taken to help address some of these problems. South Cardiff continues to benefit from European Objective Two funding, supporting a range of initiatives and expanding the number, type and range of jobs and training opportunities. Communities in Butetown, Splott, Ely and Caerau are also benefiting from the Welsh Assembly's 'Communities First Initiative' which aims to help build economic and social capacity

within communities to encourage renewal from the bottom up.

Cities are not islands unto themselves. To its credit, however, Cardiff has always been acutely conscious of its coalfield heritage and its economic links with the Valleys. If inter-dependence has been the abiding theme of the relationship between Cardiff and the Valleys, its nature changed radically when the fortunes of the city and the region began to diverge after 1920. That is when the economic flows from north to south changed. No longer was coal moving in that direction it was people in search of jobs.

> They dug for coal as if there were no tomorrow, as if it and the 'prosperity' it brought would last forever. For decades, Merthyr was the most intensively mined area in the world. What it cost in human terms beggars belief. Every six hours a miner was killed while working the seams of the 'Black Klondyke.' Every two minutes one was injured. The toll above ground was equally shocking. Because the waters of the River Taff were diverted to drive steam engines, the river became an open sewer and outbreaks of cholera and typhoid were frequent. By the middle of the 19th Century, 60 percent of all burials in Merthyr Tydfil were of children under the age of five. So much for the 'good old days'
>
> **MIKE UNGERSMA**
> CARDIFF: CELEBRATION FOR A CITY
> (HACKMAN, 1999)

Although Cardiff and the Valleys continued to be inter-dependent after the decline of the coal export trade, the centre of economic gravity shifted decisively from the coalfield to the coast. It took politicians rather longer to realise the fact, still longer to accept it. Far from celebrating the growing inter-dependence between the city and the region, successive political leaders in the Valleys expressed deep misgivings about the growing divergence in the economic fortunes of the coalfield and the coast. Imagining regional development to be a zero sum game where there is only one winner, they tend to

see Cardiff's gains as the Valley's losses, even though their labour markets are increasingly one and the same. This attitude helps to explain the concern in parts of the Valleys, especially along the Heads of the Valleys, to the development of Cardiff Bay. "What's in it for us?," they asked. "Cardiff gets it all." The Cardiff Bay Development Corporation and its chairman, Geoffrey Inkin, tried time and again to persuade Valleys' leaders that the region as a whole would benefit. In a tour of Valley authorities in 1991, for example, he told his audience:

'We look on the regeneration of Cardiff Bay not only as bringing a new era of sustained prosperity for the people of Cardiff, but for the economic benefits to be shared with the people of the Valleys.'

At that time some 27,000 commuters a day travelled into Cardiff from the Valleys to the north and north-west of the capital. By 2002 this figure had increased to 36,000 underlining the growing integration of the labour markets of the former coalfield and the coast. Today more than a third, or 70,000, of Cardiff's workforce commutes into the city from south Wales and beyond. These travel-to-work patterns reveal part of the dynamic inter-connections between seemingly disparate places in the region. They are not always apparent because of arbitrary local authority boundaries. Unquestionably, the Vale and Valleys are becoming more and more dependent on Cardiff's urban labour market, highlighting the role that cities throughout the European Union play as drivers of regional growth.

'Cardiff should do for Wales what other capital cities do for their nations. It must serve as the capital for Wales, as well as the capital of Wales.'

Should commuting increase, and it is almost certain to do so, it will put intolerable pressure on roads like the A470. This makes it an imperative that the city and region design a better and more sustainable transport system. Arguably, the creation of a mass transit system, embracing all of south Wales, is the biggest and most important planning challenge of the decade.

If the city is now and forever linked to the Valleys, the relationship between it and the nation becomes even more complicated. It was the political interplay between the city and the nation that helped Cardiff to reinvent itself with a triple dividend: firstly by becoming

the capital of Wales in 1955; secondly by reaping the benefits of administrative devolution after the establishment of the Welsh Office in 1964; and thirdly by becoming the official 'seat of government' in Wales following the creation of the National Assembly in 1999. The benefits are immense, and are seen in the concentration of public administration employees in the capital, underlining the fact that Cardiff is a huge beneficiary of the political devolution from Whitehall to Wales. And just as we see recommendations that civil service jobs be de-centralised from London to the regions, the Welsh Assembly Government is seeking to do the same in Wales, beginning with its Regeneration and

Social Justice department, parts of which are being relocated to Merthyr.

Forging a better relationship between the nation and the capital is key to the success of Cardiff. There is a need for a more strategic approach to managing the relationship between the nation and its capital. In its 2004 White Paper on the future of Cardiff: Building For Our Future the Council stated that 'Cardiff should do for Wales what other capital cities do for their nations. It must serve as the capital *for* Wales, as well as the capital *of* Wales.'

> If London is successful in its bid for the Olympic Games, Cardiff will share the glory of offering the Millennium Stadium as one of the main venues. This magnificent structure does represent the passion and ambition of the Welsh.
>
> **HELEN PONTING**
> 'JUST CAPITAL' IN LIVING FOR RETIREMENT

All of this suggests the relationship between the nation and its capital needs to be addressed in a more strategic fashion. It is a new role for Cardiff – its triple status – and it is still learning what is expected of a capital. It seems genuinely committed to doing more but it needs more help. The great, world-attracting events it hosts – the European Summit in 1998, the 1999 Rugby World Cup and the FA Cup – have done much to promote Cardiff and Wales to a wider international audience. Now, the new Wales Millennium Centre will raise that image even higher in Wales and beyond.

But grand events are not the only way in which Cardiff can be a more effective capital for Wales. Less noticeable, but no less important, is the way in which Cardiff is consciously trying to become an urban window on rural produce, especially local food and drink. The Blas event that was held in the Old Library highlighted the way in which the city can help to promote the country by showcasing an array of high quality food and drink products from around Wales to both tourists and local people. The opening of Crockertons, a local food deli in Caroline Street, is another example of a Cardiff retailer specialising in the sale of local products from around Wales. The centenary and golden jubilee celebrations now provide a unique opportunity for Cardiff to promote local food products from all over Wales. All are daily examples of the city working for, and with, the country. But they

are also examples of the capital taking the lead in delivering sustainable development because, by fostering local food chains, it is promoting a whole series of other things too – like healthier products, new markets for local producers and lower 'food miles' all of which resonate with Cardiff's recently acquired status as the world's first Fairtrade Capital City. It is in these less visible and seemingly ordinary ways, as well as through major events, that Cardiff's reputation as a capital for Wales will eventually be judged.

What remains to be done? Lots. And what is exciting has to be the potential our city has to move from being a small, if dynamic provincial capital, to a European metropolis or city and region acting as an economic dynamo not just for itself and the area, but for Wales as a whole. With its increasingly attractive and expanding leisure, retailing and hospitality, Cardiff can become one of Europe's major destinations for short breaks and cultural tourism. The foundations are there for further growth in the creative industries and in the information technologies areas. These are likely to represent the key areas of growth in income and employment over the next 10 to 20 years and few cities are as well-placed to capitalise on these trends as Cardiff. Charting the course to achievement means dealing with a number of challenges.

In an increasingly competitive domestic and international economic environment, Cardiff has to sell itself more forcefully as a destination for tourists, potential new business investors and as a host for major international sporting, political and cultural events. Having the infrastructure alone is not enough - Cardiff also needs a more positive and distinctive brand but one which is rooted in the city's history and culture and owned by the people of Cardiff.

Transport improvements are critical to Cardiff's plans for expansion. The city needs an integrated mass transit system based upon improved rail links to the Valleys, more regular and well-publicised public transport links between the city centre and the Bay and airport, as well as completion of the city's outer ring road.

At the heart of the knowledge economy is the interplay between a city's higher education sector and its business community and Cardiff needs to ensure this relationship continues to generate direct and indirect economic dividends in and beyond the city.

Encouraging social enterprise and building on opportunities for developing small businesses in less prosperous communities are also important ways to create employment opportunities at the other end of the social spectrum. Making Dumballs Road a hub for music studios to develop better links with established multi-media industries is just one example. Support for indigenous food and catering outlets, building on the success of the Old Library, Crockertons and the Riverside Farmers Market, is another. Cardiff also needs to tap the potential of its public sector budgets in order to promote local produce.

Cardiff's future growth is not only dependent upon continued public-private collaboration but also requires the full involvement of its communities. This will help to develop the self-confidence of the city and its inhabitants and the development of an agenda shared by the many, not just the few. This means close Council co-operation with the National Assembly for Wales and with other local authorities to fulfil its expanded role in the region.

Cardiff can become one of Europe's major destinations for short breaks and cultural tourism

Sian Love
Teacher of
Welsh at
Corpus Christi
High School

" I think Welsh is becoming far more important, especially in pushing educational standards higher. With Welsh at primary school level, the number of speakers is increasing. The jobs pages of the Western Mail are full of jobs where speaking Welsh is an advantage, or for those who are willing to learn. Children know today it is a core, required subject, and most of them – 90 per cent – seem happy to get on and do it.

We have a strong sense of community in Wales based on our identity. Wales has a rich culture. Years ago it was forbidden to speak Welsh – the 'Welsh not'. Our willingness to cling to our culture and our language makes us stronger. I learnt Welsh as a second language from the age of 11. I never thought I would be teaching it some day.

While rugby is a national symbol in Wales, we can't all play the game. But we can all learn Welsh and it is moving from strength to strength. Welsh is at the core of our identity just as it is for any nationality. It has never been more important than now. "

"Here at 'C2C' it may look like a call centre but we are taking calls, not making them. When people dial 029 2087 2087, this is where their call comes through. Council Tax, housing benefits, street lighting — most calls to do with Council services come to us.

Our internal computer system gives us tonnes of information so that we can answer questions quickly. We're not here just as a referral centre but to take action where we can. Say a street light is out. On my computer I can zoom in on a map of the particular street and even the light to get its unique reference number and then put through the request to have it dealt with. So, whether it is about a street light or council taxes, we try to deal with it here, directly.

I've been here for nearly a year and I feel really proud that I am representing the city to the people of Cardiff. We're here to solve problems, not pass them along. In the past, people looked through the phone book, saw the long list of council departments and thought: 'Where do I start?' Now all it takes to 'Connect to Cardiff' is one number or an email."

Tony Burnel
Customer
Services
Representati
at C2C

The Environmental Transformation of Cardiff

Chapter 2

Adapted from text by Richard Cowell & Neil Harris

We have a duty
and responsibility
to find more
sustainable ways
of living our lives
and conducting
our business.

Local Sustainability
Strategy for Cardiff

Maps of Cardiff from 30 years ago show a place still instantly recognisable, with its 'fan-like' structure reaching out from its dockland core towards suburbia. Cardiff is small and compact, with its dense streets of Victorian terraced housing encircling the city centre. Post-war suburbs stretch northwards, while major council housing estates flank the city east and west.

Look closer however, and the modern city starts to take on a different shape. New roads encircle the city, linked to out of town shopping centres. Designer apartments have replaced the wasteland that was the former docklands, while new housing estates extend to the boundaries of the city. The network of parks and open spaces flourish, while the pollutants of heavy industry – sulphurous haze in the air and coal dust in the Taff and Rhymney – have gone with the industries that created them. The city is visibly greener. Yet Cardiff now faces new environmental and land use issues as it fulfils its role as a capital city. As it changes, so too do the pressures on its environment and the quality of life of its residents, presenting future generations with a whole new series of challenging questions.

South Wales now began to experience a great exodus, and by 1950 it was estimated that a staggering 400,000 people had abandoned the great coal valleys.

CARDIFF: CELBRATION FOR A CITY
MIKE UNGERSMA

Anybody visiting Cardiff today will witness first hand how the city has been transformed. It continues with Cardiff proclaiming itself as one of Europe's fastest growing capitals. This ambition echoes the grandiose predictions of city planners in the 1960s, when Cardiff was expected to double in size to 500,000 people before the end of the century. Yet the 1960s vision of a modern and greatly expanded Cardiff did not materialise. Not only did the city fail in its aspiration to grow, its population went into decline. The 1981 census actually recorded a fall in Cardiff's population of some three percent from 1971. A 'low cost, no growth' strategy was forced on the city, reinforced by wider social and economic changes. Cardiff's population reached 297,000 by 1991, reflecting modest growth during the 1980s and, more significantly, reversing the decline witnessed in the 1970s. The city that had exploded on to the scene in the nineteenth century with incredible population growth, had gone into decline, then stagnated, before making a modest recovery by 1991. The development of large council housing estates in St Mellons and Ely formed the Eastern and Western extremes of a 'Southern Arc' of relatively deprived communities which included those parts of the city centre comprising row after row of terraced housing largely built during the late 19th and early 20th Centuries. Stark changes took place in some of these communities, population densities declined in some places as families moved out to the new housing estates on the city's fringe.

I think it is fairly safe to say that the upper limit on what is desirable for the size of a city is something of the order of a half a million inhabitants. It is quite clear that above such a size nothing is added to the virtue of a city....the finest cities in history have been very small by 20th Century standards.

SMALL IS BEAUTIFUL: ECONOMICS AS IF PEOPLE MATTERED
E. F. SCHUMACHER (PERENNIAL, 1989)

By the 1970s, the social costs of this large-scale redevelopment were clearly evident, and the clearance of housing simply to enhance traffic capacity became unacceptable – socially, economically and environmentally. The emphasis shifted to renewal rather than clearance, but implementation proved slow. Inner Cardiff of the 1980s still possessed a housing stock dating predominantly from before the First World War. And as the decades elapsed, the social impact of relocating people to new

estates also began to emerge. The city's 'peripheral estates', including Ely, Llanrumney and St. Mellons, which contrast sharply with some of the other, more affluent parts of the city, became home to some three quarters of the city's unemployed. Cardiff remained a city sharply divided along socio-economic lines.

So, Cardiff – unlike many cities across the UK – did not grow significantly during the 1970s and 1980s, but curiously, this did not halt expansion into the surrounding countryside. Significant extensions were made to Cardiff's suburbs as development crept outwards to the north of the city. Villages within the Cardiff fringe, such as Radyr, were rapidly engulfed by 1970s residential development. One account describes how 'farms, hamlets and villages which were once thought to be deep in the countryside were swallowed up and their names given to new housing estates'. Major housing developments proceeded apace at Thornhill in the late 1970s and later at Pentwyn, fuelling concerns over the physical limits to Cardiff's expansion and presenting very real dilemmas of development versus conservation.

> Cardiff gives the visitor an impression of modernity and progressiveness, of spacious streets and buildings, of docks and ships, and of great commercial activity which well merit the epithet of 'the Chicago of Wales'. It is both ancient and modern, Celtic and cosmopolitan, progressive, wealthy, enterprising, and a centre of learning.
>
> **THE CARDIFF TIMES**
> APRIL 1905

As it expanded Cardiff increasingly pressed upon long-standing geographical boundaries and landscapes widely seen as sacred. Early attempts in the 1960s to constrain expansion through an informal green belt enjoyed mixed success, but it was held back by the sea to the south, Caerphilly and Garth Mountains to the north and steep hills

to the west. So the city looked east, encouraging developments that threatened to create a coastal urban sprawl from Barry in the west to Newport and perhaps even Chepstow in the east. But that would mean encroaching on the valuable wetland environment of the Wentloog Levels. However, more than just landscape was at stake. As far back as the 1960s, Cardiff's model of urban development – the incremental extension of its fringes – was recognised as one which it would be difficult to connect through an effective public transport system. To this day, it is still the pattern for Cardiff's growth, with all the attendant problems of high car use and congestion.

Investment in major new roads over the past 30 years has changed not only the way the city appears on maps, but also people's experiences of Cardiff. Two major pieces of road infrastructure have significantly re-shaped the city. The first, the M4 motorway, was opened to traffic along its length in 1980. It had a paradoxical effect on the city's urban form. On the one hand, the M4 marks the 'natural' limit to Cardiff's northward expansion, protecting the lower reaches of Caerphilly Mountain and the green backdrop to views from the south of the city. On the other hand, the M4 has exerted a gravitational pull on the location of new industry and other forms of new development such as housing and retail, as developers seek to take advantage of new, strategic opportunities in the M4 corridor.

Just as important is the Peripheral Distributor Road – known to most as the Ely Link Road - which connects the west of Cardiff into the heart of Cardiff Bay. It was to be a 'necklace of opportunity' central to the docks' redevelopment, but unexpected cost meant the road was a long time coming. It was first unveiled by the County Council nearly 30 years ago as an alternative to earlier proposals for roads that would have driven their way through Cardiff's inner city. The last section to be built, which passes through a tunnel in the centre of the Cardiff Bay development, was completed in 1995. An earlier plan would have cut directly through Butetown, requiring a number of listed Georgian buildings to be demolished. The Cardiff Bay Development Corporation – responsible for the docklands renewal – decided that a tunnel, even though more expensive, would be far less disruptive. But the 'necklace' remains incomplete, awaiting funding that will allow the expensive eastern connection to the M4 to be built.

Cardiff has experienced significant growth in the ownership and use of private cars over the past 30 years, enabling people to live at some distance from where they work. Processes of counter-urbanisation, evident in Cardiff since the 1960s, witnessed people moving out to surrounding areas, including Llantrisant, Caerphilly and the rural Vale of Glamorgan. How best to address the inexorable rise in commuting traffic coming into the city has formed part of Cardiff's planning policy agenda since the mid-1970s. Various measures have been promoted. Urban traffic control systems were successfully introduced to the city in 1976 in order to ease congestion, and proposals for a system of tolls were considered but not implemented. Efforts have been made to ensure all major new housing developments are serviced by public transport, and Cardiff's first bus lane was designated along St. Mary Street in 1975. Yet such measures did not prove sufficient to reverse long-term decline in the use of bus services.

The British are a deeply suburban people. We dislike cities and like detached houses. The car has fuelled this taste dramatically, and given us expanded and rambling towns and villages. Their inhabitants work in green-field factories (necessary not least for ease of one-floor operation by forklift trucks and other industrial machines), and shop in huge out-of-town supermarkets.

This "urban" scene is not merely expanding the element of the urban in our lives. One of its features is a curious uniformity, never before sensed so powerfully. We fear that Britain is in danger of becoming monotonous, a place in which uniform architecture and infrastructure spreads as a blight.

RICHARD D. NORTH
LIFE ON A MODERN PLANET
(MANCHESTER UNIVERSITY PRESS, 1995)

The promotion of rail services in Cardiff has been a relative success story. Passenger numbers on the Valley Lines increased by over half between 1983 and 1988 following significant investments in new routes, new stations and park and ride facilities. Cardiff's geography also lends itself to cycling, and a network of dedicated cycle routes has developed since 1982.

Like all cities, Cardiff has had to accommodate the changing requirements of business, commerce and industry. Industry and warehousing were decanted out of the city centre in the early 1970s to make space for shopping and commerce. Closure of the East Moors Steel Works in 1978 opened up new possibilities for development of the southern waterfront for manufacturing and other industrial uses. Yet the city's economy was changing and the docklands – traditionally seen as a 'backyard' area for industry, manufacturing and port-related activities – showed signs of emerging as a commercial area to challenge the city centre as a location for office development. The former South Glamorgan County Council boldly demonstrated its commitment to the regeneration of Cardiff's docklands by moving in 1988 to its new offices at the edge of Bute East Dock, now Atlantic Wharf.

Industrial land made way for offices and commercial development, reflecting the changing economy of the city. The changing demands of industry has had important land-use consequences over the past 20 years. New land has been

Cardiff has made much of its legacy of Victorian and Edwardian parks and open spaces

allocated to meet business demands for large, flat sites, with high accessibility and ready availability. Parcels of land have been allocated for 'special employment use' in the past - many of them adjacent to the city's new strategic roads – only to remain undeveloped for long periods of time during economic recession. The Council put up a determined, but ultimately unsuccessful, fight to resist the loss of these sites in the 1980s against a trend for out-of-town retail development. Culverhouse Cross Retail Park stands out today as one of the city's finest testaments to the inability of planners and politicians to anticipate the changing demands of industry and commerce. The consequences for traffic generation were, alas, all too accurately anticipated.

The legacy of hazardous industry and waste became one of the principal concerns in the regeneration of the waterfront in the early 1980s, prompting the first waste policies for the city. Prior to this, waste was dealt with on an ad hoc, 'end of the pipe' basis. True, the city enjoyed sporadic recycling initiatives, but the twenty years that elapsed since 1975 saw Cardiff's predicament worsen. The problem was the amount of waste produced in Cardiff kept on growing relentlessly, more than doubling from the early 1980s to approximately 1 million tonnes per year during the late 1990s, ranging from inert materials to highly toxic chemical by-products and residues.

> When the archaeologists of the future look at the deposits of the last 250 years, they will find a biological discontinuity as big as any in the past. They will expose a richness not of fossils but plastic bags and other human refuse.
>
> **SIR CRISPIN TICKELL**
> GREEN COLLEGE, OXFORD

Domestic waste also became a more significant part with biodegradable waste from households, once dumped into landfill sites, creating particular risks of methane and leaking chemicals. By the time local authorities began to look seriously at the alternatives, such as recycling or incineration, Lamby Way had become the city's only active landfill site tucked away in the east 'hidden' from most of Cardiff's residents.

Cardiff has made much of its legacy of Victorian and Edwardian parks and open spaces. They are one of the city's most distinctive features and truly worthy of any capital city. Nearly 2.5 million visits are made each year to Roath Park, marking it out as the city's most popular park. Informal green spaces now also complement these formal parks. A series of local nature reserves designated between 1977 and 1995 provide protection to popular wildlife habitats, and the long-recognised potential of the river corridors to provide a network of open space 'penetrating right to the heart of the city' began to be realised, starting with the Taff Trail cycle path in 1983. Today, thousands use it every day to cycle to work or for pleasure. Caerphilly Mountain, a key element of the city's physical context, has long been recognised both for its special landscape value and its potential as a regional park. While Cardiff's residents enjoy a generous availability of green space, they are not equally accessible to all, and the inner urban areas of Adamsdown and Splott have historically fallen well below accepted standards of open space provision. Into the mid-1990s, large areas of inner Cardiff and Cardiff Bay continued to be deficient in open space, and difficulties still continue in ensuring the equitable provision of open space across the city.

> But look! Here come more crowds, pacing straight for the water, and seemingly bound for a dive. Nothing will content them but the extremist limit of the land.
>
> **HERMAN MELVILLE**
> MOBY DICK

The calm waters of Cardiff Bay today scarcely hint at the intense conflict once centred on the barrage;

The lifestyles of Cardiff residents mean they each use more than two an a half times their fair 'Earthshare' of global environmental resources

a 15 - year fracas that quite unintentionally placed the city on the international stage. The concept of a barrage across the Taff and Ely Rivers emerged as interest in the Bay gathered pace. Earlier and more modest proposals for a Taff barrage, running parallel to the distributor road and its tunnel, were pushed outwards to the mouth of the estuary as part of Cardiff Bay Development Corporation's proposals. This dramatic engineering intervention to construct a permanent, non-tidal waterfront for Cardiff, was seen as essential for attracting investment, and to prevent the Bay remaining what it had been for decades: a maritime wasteland and ghost-town. For some, however, the large expanses of tidal mudflats and bird populations had a drama of their own, and the consequences of damming two rivers in the heart of the city was simply not environmentally acceptable. From its inception in 1987 to its formal opening in 2001, the barrage conflict drew in local residents, politicians, conservation experts, environmental groups and European Union Commissioners.

> In many cases, the renewal of a key area of a city acts as a focus for national and international attention, as well as generating civic pride and a buzz that a city is on the move.
>
> **NICK BROOKE**
> FORMER PRESIDENT, ROYAL INSTITUTE OF
> CHARTERED SURVEYORS

Parliamentary approval for the barrage was only secured on the proviso that the Cardiff Bay Development Corporation would successfully manage the environmental consequences. The greatest fear was from flooding. What would be the risk of impounding a huge lake of fresh water from the Taff and Ely behind the barrage? After all, Grangetown was badly flooded in 1979, and while new flood defences had been built, could they cope this new risk? The answer was an extensive groundwater survey to assess the impact of impoundment on properties in south Cardiff. The new lake is also carefully monitored to assess its ability to hold runoff from the two rivers. One less visible by-product of the barrage has been the millions of pounds invested through Welsh Water, to divert the numerous sewage outflows that used to discharge into the Taff and Ely through new treatment works, and out into the Severn.

One factor intensifying the barrage conflict was its coincidence with a wider upsurge in public concern for the environment.

There were worries about the rate of Cardiff's expansion, loss of open space, increased road traffic and deterioration in air quality. These pressures, coupled with global debates about the sustainability of development, encouraged Cardiff City Council to improve its green credentials. In 1993, Cardiff became involved in a high profile pilot project by the International Council for Local Environmental Initiatives to design indicators of sustainability, and the city was an early signatory to the Aalborg Charter of European Cities and Towns Towards Sustainability. However, this flurry of innovation was followed by a period of treading water in the mid-1990s.

Cardiff – like so many cities - has aspired to becoming 'greener' for a decade. That commitment is reflected in the Council's treatment of environmental issues. Its 'Local Sustainability Strategy' was published in 2000, and emphasises the need to begin with the Council itself, hoping it can set an example for everyone. And since it spends £13 million on fuel alone every year, the Council clearly has potential to make a big impact. The determination to be a beacon of best environmental practice was evidenced by a wide range of initiatives – including Fair Trade Capital status, sustainable procurement and energy efficiency – all of which are woven into the core governing structures of the Council through the work of its Sustainable Development Unit and a 'sustainability advocate' in each service department.

Measured against other European urban centres, Cardiff is still categorised as a small to medium sized city

The timing was crucial since the intervening years have also seen the deepening of many environmental problems, some of them a consequence of the kind of consumer-based growth that Cardiff, like many other cities, has sought to encourage. The lifestyles of Cardiff residents mean they each use more than two and a half times their fair 'Earthshare' of global environmental resources. Tackling these issues is challenging because many solutions are out of the Council's reach and because they confront ingrained political and social priorities. Little wonder then that the city's present position combines progress with predicament.

Political visions of Cardiff's future have shown a perhaps unhealthy obsession with size. The Council's '2020' vision project – an attempt to plan for change and growth into the next decade – concluded that Cardiff was 'simply too small' for 'the Premier Division of European capitals', and needed to expand its administrative boundaries and population in order to compete.

> Our search for the essence of competitiveness is routing us away from the traditional city to the fast, vibrant, technology-rich city of the future, where urbanisation and information go hand-in-hand to create new city forms and functions. We all may be a little surprised about the future identity of at least some of the world's winning cities of the 21st Century.
>
> **ROSEMARY FEENAN**
> JONES LANG LASALLE

Measured against other European urban centres, Cardiff is still categorised as a small to medium sized city, and in terms of population just sneaks into the largest 200 cities in Europe. Nevertheless, the city is expected to continue the trend of population growth witnessed in recent years. From an official population total of 310,000 in 2001, it has been projected that by 2016 the city could boast as many as 350,000 residents. This rate of growth continues a trend witnessed throughout the 1990s but masked by a questionable 2001 Census population figure.

Could further growth and population increase threaten the long-recognised qualities of the city? To many people, the city's compact size makes it attractive and gives it some of the character and feel of a village. About a third of Cardiff's land area remains as countryside - one of its less well known qualities - but over the

next few decades those areas may face their greatest development pressures, as planners balance proposals for a green belt around the north and east of the city with options for accommodating growing household numbers. While current plans propose 60 percent of new housing be built on brownfield or previously-developed land, much of which will be located in the Bay, some 6,000 new houses are still destined for greenfield sites on Cardiff's fringe. Will existing open spaces within the city be considered free from development pressure? The current controversy over housing proposals for Llanishen Reservoir is a prime example of the pressures Cardiff will increasingly face.

City leaders now embrace the importance of environmental enhancement for Cardiff's future economic competitiveness and social well-being, and it features in the Community Strategy, Better Communities, Brighter Lives. Recently, most efforts have been focused on improving parks, green belts and fighting the ever-present problem of litter leaving battles about the environmental consequences of expansion, consumerism, and of attracting affluent consumers and tourists, to be fought out in other arenas. Balancing global environmental risks against its ambitions will become a fundamental challenge for Cardiff as it moves deeper into the 21st Century.

One issue is rising traffic, which increasingly congests Cardiff's streets and causes pollution on a local and global scales. It is true that more people walk and cycle to work in Cardiff that other communities in Wales, but this must be set against rising traffic volumes. Figures for Cardiff show that while the average Cardiffian walks just a half-mile each day, 70,000 others travel into the city each day, and seven out of ten of those journeys are made by car. Car usage is at a level where it is beginning to impede accessibility and the economic development of the city, and pollution, traffic congestion and accidents caused by vehicles are at an unacceptable level. Indeed the pollution from cars, buses and lorries prompted the Council to designate four 'Air Quality Management Areas' – sections of the city where pollutants can reach dangerous levels if remedial action is not taken. And, like hundreds of cities around the world, worse is to come, with the likelihood of up to 30 per cent more vehicles on Cardiff's roads by 2010.

> No one is going to give up their car.
>
> **MARGARET THATCHER**

Sustainable transport is rising up the city agenda, but taking action is difficult, in Cardiff and everywhere else. The Council faces a difficult challenge between not forcing people out of their cars while relying on sufficient improvement in public transport to encourage people to vote with their feet. Its 2003 White Paper on transport identified a £400 million capital programme to complete the docklands freeway to the M4 in the east, various link roads and interchanges, expand the heavy

rail network, and develop express bus routes, cycle routes and pedestrianisation. Funding is proposed to come from a public-private partnership using a mix of charges, parking and development levies.

While this is bold and innovative thinking, the impact of improving public transport can too easily be overestimated. After all, Cardiff experienced a 22 per cent drop in public transport journeys to work between 1991 and 2001, and a third of Cardiff's population never uses public transport, while a further third do so only occasionally. Furthermore, one in five of the city's 130,000 households have two or more cars. The city's pattern of development may be worsening the problem. The dispersion of retail and leisure facilities, initially foisted on the Council following planning inquiries but now deemed to be essential to successful major projects – whether that is the International Sports Village, the new Cardiff City Football Stadium or opening up the south side of Roath Basin – will further increase the temptation to drive. Indeed, Cardiff Bay, where developer preferences for extensive car parking repeatedly overrode strategic traffic concerns, is a major offender. Across Britain and throughout the industrial world, no greater challenge faces politicians than persuading drivers to give up driving.

What to do with waste – still another chronic problem of the modern city. Cardiff is no different. At the current rate of dumping, the Lamby Way landfill will be full by 2010. And the pressure from Brussels demanding a reduction in the land filling of waste further limits room for

manoeuvre. Encouragingly, two thirds of municipal solid waste is potentially capable of being composted or recycled, and the city is starting to regain the initiative. After the hesitant introduction of a 'green bag' recycling scheme in 1998, the more recent 'Bin and Box' project has accelerated recycling rates in the areas where it has been introduced. But the challenge is stiff. While Cardiff's rates of recycling have increased year on year, from three-and-a-half per cent in 2000, to nearly 10 per cent in 2002, the city lags behind the Welsh average and is way behind comparable European cities. Moreover, improvements in recycling rates are being outpaced by increases in the amount of waste produced in the city, which is increasing by five per cent each year. Tackling waste generation is the crux of the problem, and here city-level action depends significantly on its citizens, its businesses, and on national and European regulation. Unless Cardiff's residents and businesses are able to reduce the amount of waste they create, they will be forced to address unpalatable and expensive alternatives.

If the challenges of transport and waste are shared by other cities, not so the unique test of dealing with a freshwater lake in Cardiff Bay – at once a remarkable amenity, the quality of which is central to Cardiff's regeneration, and a complex conjunction of environmental responsibilities. As the dust settles on

the barrage conflict, so the longer-term consequences are clearer. On the groundwater front, by 2004 only one property of the 23,000 in south Cardiff deemed at risk from rising groundwater had been damaged. Pumping oxygen into the lake has created a flourishing coarse fishery. The equally flourishing populations of midges, algae and invasive Canadian Pondweed are hopefully temporary residents. If numerous common bird species have made their homes in the Bay, conservationists were also broadly correct about the displacement or disappearance of the vulnerable water bird populations that used to winter on the mudflats. To those responsible for it, what marks out the Bay as an environmental management challenge is more than the sum of its parts. The scale and novelty of the task of managing such a vast artificial inland lake means, as one conservation officer put it, that "there are issues where we're at the leading edge of technology, meaning we've had to be very innovative". Not for the first time, Cardiff's future success is bound up with a wider Wales. To maintain the water quality means working with the Valleys to clean up water flowing into the Bay. And it means asking the Welsh Assembly to allow sufficient funding to make sure that environmental quality is maintained so that future generations may also enjoy it.

Managing the environment has become far more complex, both as expectations of quality have increased, and as key players look beyond simple technical fixes to tackling problems at their source – whether they come from developers or consumers. If Cardiff's residents are beginning to recognise the importance of the environment to their daily lives, there is no room for complacency, and fundamental changes are needed. The challenges are daunting but manageable.

Past exercises in developing a future vision for Cardiff have not adequately addressed the emerging environmental awareness of residents.

People increasingly look to public authorities to demonstrate political leadership in addressing environmental challenges

The consequences of pursuing relentless growth have been ignored or at least underplayed. These must be made clear. People increasingly look to public authorities to demonstrate political leadership in addressing environmental challenges. Cardiff's Community Strategy goes a long way towards bringing sustainable development issues to the fore, even if it is presently preoccupied with litter and parks. Now, planning policies must also respond. At the same time, there are limits to what councils can do to address environmental problems. Such measures need support from everyone – businesses as well as citizens. But in both cases it means adapting lifestyles to a new reality, and that is no small undertaking. Balancing messages that promote alternatives to the car with messages that allow retail and leisure facilities swathes of free car parking have to be reconciled. Could change come about through the development of 'eco-communities' as demonstration projects, piecing together sustainable lifestyles in targeted areas of the city? For some, education is the answer. For others, taxes will be required to achieve the needed change in people's behaviour.

Over recent years local organisations have engaged in extensive discussions about the future of Cardiff. The local community planning process has developed as a key arena of debate about local issues. We believe that by working together we can and will make measurable progress to better communities and brighter lives.

CARDIFF COMMUNITY STRATEGY

Cardiff's expansion is pressing on many of the 'natural' boundaries that defined it for much of its history. For some, it is enough to remain a 'small and beautiful' capital. For them, the advantages of growth are not obvious. Others see growth as both desirable and inevitable. Whatever the view, if its pattern of present growth continues, it means moving beyond present boundaries. There are no easy choices, but any decision needs to keep sustainability at the forefront. The ability to achieve more sustainable suburbs may shortly be tested with the 4,000 new dwellings currently proposed

for south of the M4 at Pontprennau and Lisvane, a step based partly on public transport improvements. In future, might it be necessary to return to the possibility that Cardiff's growth cannot be accommodated within the county area? Would this be more preferable in environmental or social terms than continued expansion 'at the edges'? Another alternative to peripheral expansion is greater density of population. That is already happening in the city centre, with clear benefits of reducing pressure on greenfield land, avoiding the need for car journeys and revitalising the core of the city.

The problem of the growing use of cars can no longer be ignored. The scale of investment required to deal with Cardiff's transport issues is significant, and the move to the centre – while helpful – is not a long-term answer. The challenges are clear: how to effectively and equitably regulate personal car use, to deal with potential changes as new transport infrastructure is put in place, and to balance all with the need for an economic engine to provide prosperity for all? Budget restrictions on local authorities mean major new projects

inevitably require a significant injection of private capital, bringing with it more retail and leisure spin-offs. That in turn, at least in the past, has meant more dispersal – and more car travel.

The city has started to make real progress in the recovery and recycling of waste. It now needs to take the lead in helping businesses and residents reduce the amount of waste they produce in the first place. Cardiff's shrinking capacity for landfill and tipping make this an especially pressing concern. It is likely that the city will in any case be forced to consider alternative means of waste disposal, including shipping it to another region, or energy-from-waste schemes – all controversial and expensive. As with traffic issues, the case for cooperation with other local authorities becomes stronger, but the stakes become higher. There are also questions of how sustainable behaviour may be built into the city's very urban fabric, notably designing housing estates around the efficient use of green energy and waste recovery. The scope for tidal power within the barrage has already been investigated, and burning wood waste washed into the Bay is under development. Given demanding targets for renewable energy across all of Wales, might not the Cardiff sea front provide a site for wind farms rather than the Welsh countryside, as takes place in the urban settings of Rotterdam or Amsterdam?

One of Cardiff's key dilemmas in envisioning its future is to reconcile the city's development with its wetlands, including the remaining tidal waterfronts – the Severn and the Rhymney – and the traditionally inaccessible Wentloog Levels. These have been sites of land-use conflict in the past, and the pressure will not go away. At the same time, tidal habitats have become increasingly valuable for birds displaced from Cardiff Bay, and are now protected under stringent European directives. Can the city embrace wetland landscapes as an ecological asset that needs space to function, rather than constrain and erode them

Climate change will leave few aspects of Cardiff life unaffected, from our parks and gardens to our lifestyles, wildlife, and the design of our buildings

through new development? The question raises practical and perceptual challenges for Cardiff. Can a city that has traditionally treated its mudflats as 'wasteland' start positively embracing Cardiff's image as a 'city that floats'? Can the ecological and cultural distinctiveness of these green spaces be maintained in the face of unrelenting pressure to maximise the use of every inch? What might be the benefits of embracing these 'fluid' spaces – the rivers of Cardiff – as spaces that bridge the old and tiresome psychological barriers between north and south Cardiff, and that can provide access to greenspace, healthy recreation opportunities and amenities for all.

If some environmental issues present the city with difficult choices, others face it with little choice other than to adapt. Such is the case with climate change – even with greater efforts to cut greenhouse gas emissions, Cardiff along with the rest of the UK is still likely to face a series of climatically-induced challenges. Global warming is predicted to mean hotter, drier summers, wetter winters and stormier weather overall. While the Bay and barrage are designed to reduce flood risks, including some allowance for climate

change and sea level rise, forecasts indicate that sewer and drainage systems will be at greater risk of being overwhelmed by flood events. Rising sea levels will put further pressure on estuary habitats beyond Cardiff's sea wall. Cardiff residents will literally feel the heat. Climate change will leave few aspects of Cardiff life unaffected, from our parks and gardens to our lifestyles, wildlife and the design of our buildings. Thinking forward to 2025 is clearly insufficient: the challenge of 'climate-proofing' Cardiff means casting our vision much further ahead.

> As politicians, organisations and individuals we have a duty and responsibility to find more sustainable ways of living our lives and conducting our business. There are no easy solutions. In the rush of our daily lives and with the demands, needs and wants of modern society, it is easy for us all to ignore the bigger and longer term picture.
>
> **CARDIFF COUNCIL'S
> SUSTAINABILITY STRATEGY FOR CARDIFF**

Rob Murphy
Youth Worker -
Llanrumney
Youth Centre

" We have 21 full-time youth centres in Cardiff and half a dozen satellite centres. I'm responsible for six of them. We work mainly with 13 to 19-year-olds. At 14, young people are making decisions about what they want to do, and at 16 it's usually an exit point from school. We're saying, 'No, it can be longer - a springboard to move on and continue your education, whether you are going the academic route or whether you want to become a good plumber or electrician.'

We are not only reinforcing messages that children hear at school. We're also working with the bottom five per cent - those at risk of being excluded or getting into trouble. It's these kids you read about in the newspapers, but they are a minority. Even in poorer areas of the city, most kids are fine. They are not born 'problem kids'. When they come here and get a Duke of Edinburgh Award, or get to see a cow in a field for the first time, or get a passport to go to Disneyland in Paris, as we did with one group of 15-year-olds – it's a pleasure to see all these things happening to kids from pretty tough backgrounds. I wouldn't want to do anything else. "

"

I've been working with the Road Safety Department for the past 27 years, as a mobile Crossing Patrol, so I can be working at any of 98 locations in Cardiff. Part of my duties also involves the training of new crossing patrols.

I originally trained as a secretary and thought that was what I wanted to be, but became a patrol when my children were in school. Because I like the contact with the children I decided to stay. In my opinion patrols play an important part of serving the community. I don't think people truly appreciate how important lollypop people are.

The work is enjoyable and rewarding and I regularly receive lots of positive feedback from children, parents and the schools.

Not very long ago, at St. Mellons, I saw this girl coming down the street with her children, and I instantly recognised her from a previous location some years before. She remembered me and I realised that I'm now escorting another generation across the road.

"

City Centre and Bay
Chapter 3

Adapted from text by John Punter

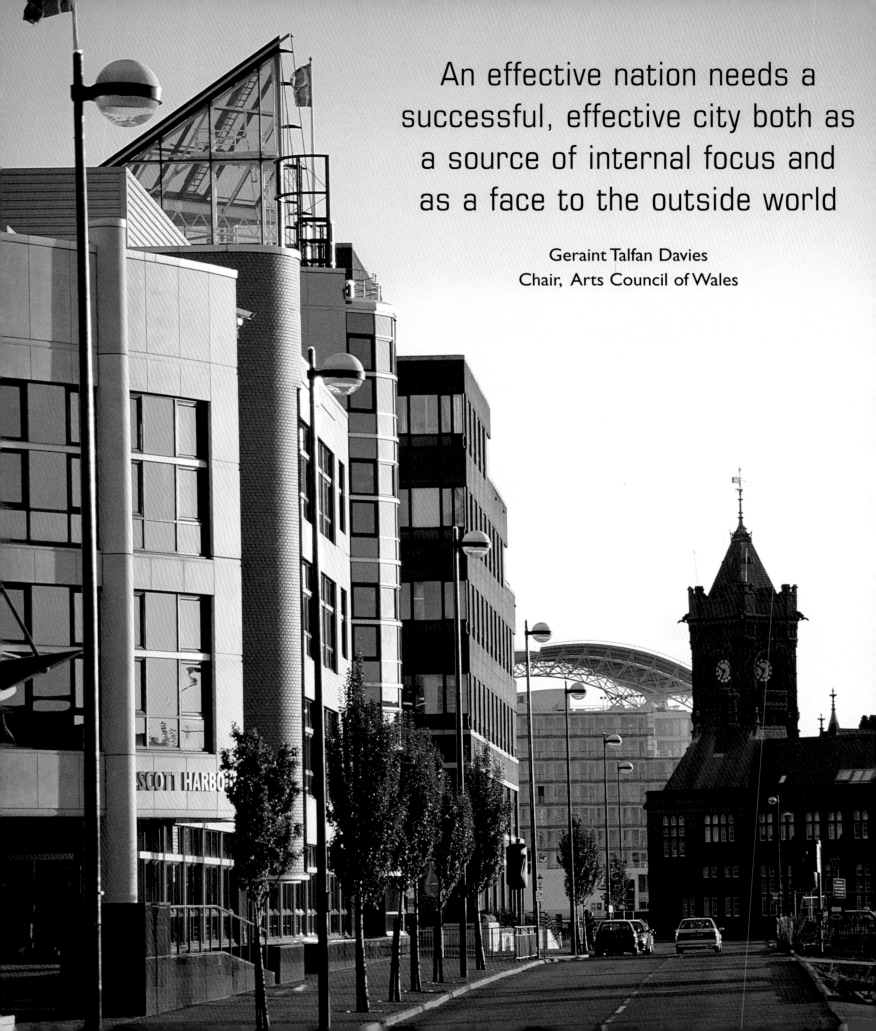

An effective nation needs a successful, effective city both as a source of internal focus and as a face to the outside world

Geraint Talfan Davies
Chair, Arts Council of Wales

The most eminent British planners of the 1960s described the city centre of Cardiff in 1964 as "worn out, inconvenient, drab and downright dangerous". Pick up a copy of the popular series of paperbacks, Cardiff Then and Now, to see what they meant. Some may find it nostalgic, but who would want to live in the dingy buildings, chaotic traffic and poor conditions for the pedestrian as well as the slum conditions and dereliction in the Docks the series portrays? While badly bombed city centres like Swansea and Bristol were redeveloped with large amounts of government money in the 1950s and 1960s, a largely unscathed Cardiff had to wait until the mid 1970s, and for private investment, to begin large-scale reconstruction. As it turned out this was something of a blessing in disguise, allowing the city to keep more of its character and old street pattern, and forcing it to pursue more modest redevelopment plans.

> Why can't we be less hypocritical and admit that the motor car is just about the most convenient device we have ever invented?
>
> **PROFESSOR SIR COLIN BUCHANAN CBE**
> TRAFFIC IN TOWNS, 1963

The city submitted its first development plan for government approval in 1953. It was rejected, and the city leaders were told "to consider seeking specialist advice on planning". This led to the establishment of a new planning department and Chief Officer, and the appointment of the nation's premier planning consultants, Colin Buchanan and Partners, to prepare a new plan.

The company's founder – Professor, later Sir Colin Buchanan – was one of the first professional planners in the UK to become interested in the dangers and problems of traffic. Hence, it came as no surprise that Buchanan and his associates applied their unique brand of transport-driven land use planning and post war boom-driven growth projections to create a stunning vision of a new city centre. This stretched as far north as Maindy Stadium and was studded with high-rise office complexes, and criss-crossed by 'motorways' to allow people to drive in and park on the edge of the ring road, encircling a largely pedestrianised city centre. While the M4, Eastern Avenue, the western arm of the Peripheral Distributor Road, what is more commonly called the PDR or Ely Link, and the central car parks were all built broadly on Buchanan's suggested alignments, the city scrapped the rest of the proposed urban motorway network. The entire plan seemed based on Buchanan's anxiety about the car, which he called "a monster we love." Predictably, it provoked vehement local opposition.

> Cardiff dithered, thank god. In addition to the idea about the houses that would have to go, Buchanan also wanted the city to build a 10 lane highway over the shopping area! It would be decked over with a kind of donut-hole left for the tower of St. John's Church. Good sense thankfully prevailed and nothing was done.
>
> **STANLEY COX**
> SCHOOL OF ARCHITECTURE, CARDIFF UNIVERSITY

Instead, Cardiff accepted conventional streets and boulevards as the main traffic routes within the city, giving it the civility many other British provincial towns lack.

The pedestrianisation of Queen Street proceeded in three phases to the huge benefit of shoppers and retailers

As an alternative to Buchanan, 'Centreplan 70' emerged as a modernist vision of tower and slab office blocks and covered shopping centres linked with first floor pedestrian decks and walkways. It was to be built by the private developers Ravenseft Properties Ltd, years later still collaborating with Cardiff in the expansion of St David's Centre. Their architects prepared a 'flexible' conceptual plan for redevelopment. A new library, adult education centre, entertainment centre, concert hall, arts centre/theatre, exhibition conference centre, youth and design centres would be built alongside, and largely paid for by, the new retail and office space. The architects and the city planners made all the right noises about respecting the character of the city, but the only part of the centre not to be demolished was the St Mary's Street-Working Street corridor. The city held its breath as the financial deal was completed but by the time the legal agreement had been signed the 1973 property crash had made the whole scheme unprofitable.

So the property recession saved Cardiff from making the redevelopment mistakes of many other British cities, and forced it to adopt a much more piecemeal and gradual approach to redevelopment. The modest inner ring road plans were implemented in two stages, reaching around to the foot of St Mary's Street by 1978, but the western arm up Westgate Street to Castle Street has never been implemented. The pedestrianisation of Queen Street proceeded in three phases to the huge benefit of shoppers and retailers, but the removal of cars from St. Mary's Street remains a Council aspiration.

In 1975 the city advertised five separate development sites they had acquired, each with a prescribed package of commercial and public facilities, and awaited offers from private developers. The

The Council took the bold step of building its new headquarters at the southern end of the dock to reinforce this regeneration effort

most important of these was land to the south of Queen Street and Hills Street. Boots, Debenhams, and Woolworths signed up with the Heron Corporation to develop the St David's Centre creating an effective, but no means ideal, link between Queen Street and The Hayes. St David's Hall was developed within the scheme, providing the city with a vital cultural venue.

> An effective nation needs a successful, effective city both as a source of internal focus and as face to the outside world. Successful cities are also crucial to cultural development, especially in the professional arts, in a world where the public's benchmarks of quality are international. We have to understand the role of cities and our own capital, and the potential fruits of a sound relationship between the city and Wales, or else we risk stunting our economic and cultural development.
>
> **GERAINT TALFAN DAVIES**
> CHAIR, ARTS COUNCIL OF WALES

The disposal of the four remaining sites was slower and more compromised as investors and developers resisted the city's aspirations and pursued their own largely functional requirements. Oxford Arcade was extended with a multi-storey car park and a new central library developed. In a deal that required a £2.5 million grant from the Welsh Office, Holiday Inn built a 14-storey hotel – now the Marriott - bolstering conference business at St David's Hall, but demolishing half of Mill Lane in the process. On the other side of Hayes Bridge Road, Toys'R'Us developed their single-storey outlet alongside the National Ice Rink and a multi-storey car park. A third multi-storey car park was completed on Bridge Street. It took a £3 million Urban Development Grant to persuade Brent Walker to develop the 'World Trade Centre', a major arena and exhibition hall subsequently known as the Cardiff International Arena, and a new hotel - Jurys - opposite. Collectively, the quality of these developments was a disappointment, but the understandable priority was to get the new facilities built to allow the city to perform as a regional capital. In the mid 1980s developers returned to Queen Street to create three small shopping malls to make it one of the best performing retail streets in the country.

As the city considered ways of further expanding its retail appeal, and developing its tourist potential, conservation assumed greater importance. St Mary's Street and Windsor Place were designated

Conservation Areas in 1975, and Cathays Park, the Parade, remnants of Charles Street and Churchill Way and Queen Street were given this status by 1992. But only St Mary's Street had significant public funding to encourage private owners to refurbish their properties. A tourism strategy emphasised the need to reinforce and market Cardiff's 'Capital City' status internationally, to develop its function as a gateway to Wales, enhance its Welshness and improve its attractions and the length of stay of visitors. This marked the beginning of the city's international aspirations.

During the 1970s redevelopment attention began to shift away from the city centre towards the now largely derelict northern docks, particularly after the closure of the East Moors Steelworks in 1978. The East Moors Plan, unveiled in 1980, led to the development of the Ocean Park Industrial Estate. This was followed by the redevelopment of Atlantic Wharf which included a mix of housing, business, industry and hotels and the conversion of three derelict warehouses. The Council took the bold step of building its new headquarters at the southern end of the dock to reinforce this regeneration effort. Regrettably, the southern end of the Dock, and its connection to Roath Basin, were filled in by Associated British Ports to create more development land. The whole experience persuaded the Welsh Secretary of State that a more efficient mechanism was needed to drive regeneration of the Docks.

We must recognise that a city is like an organism. It needs a centre and neighbourhoods as its main components. Only well balanced cities can fulfil the conception which has its origin in the Renaissance: a place to meet people and to exchange ideas.

LORD ROGERS
DESIGNER OF THE WELSH ASSEMBLY BUILDING

Every dire consequence, from a plague of midges to an invasion of yuppies, is being predicted. If the prophets of doom are right, the yuppies will be sipping their spritzers watching the sun set on the algae-covered lake of sewage, while the existing buildings, sodden from the rising water table, sink into slime.

THE GUARDIAN, JUNE 1988

Baltimore, USA

Cardiff Bay Development Corporation (CBDC) was established at the end of 1986. The Labour - controlled Council had lobbied the Secretary of State for Wales for the establishment of a development corporation, and included in the submission was a proposal for a barrage to "enhance the opportunity and scope for the regeneration of south Cardiff". Baltimore Harbour in America was very much the model, as it was for many other cities world-wide. Unlike other development corporation designations the Council was allowed to retain development control powers creating a partnership approach to development.

CBDC was given six objectives:
• Reunite the city centre with its waterfront.
• Promote development which provides a superb environment in which people will want to live, work and play.

• Achieve the highest standards of design and quality in all types of investment.
• Bring forward a mix of development which will create a wide range of opportunities and reflect the hopes and aspirations of the communities in the area.
• Stimulate residential development which provides homes for a cross-section of the population.
• Establish the area as a recognised centre of excellence and innovation in the field of urban regeneration.

The Bay was eligible for European Regional Development Funds to assist new and expanding companies, while CBDC could acquire land, grant-aid major projects, and provide discretionary funds for a wide range of schemes. The Corporation rapidly assembled some 538 acres in the first two years of its existence, but missed the opportunity to cash in on any of the late 1980s property boom which came to an abrupt end in October 1989.

The Bay's 'unique selling point' was the vision of "a major maritime city" on a freshwater lake the rationale being the tidal mud flats of the Bay would never attract major investors, employers and tourists. The Cardiff Bay Barrage was the "essential catalyst" to job creation - an extra 16,000 jobs was forecast - but it sparked major protests on environmental grounds, and the freshwater lake took a decade to materialise.

The Corporation's regeneration strategy was intended to be a flexible 'vision' founded on a clear pattern of streets and buildings and a real sense of place. Its principal features were a new "arc of entertainment" on the Inner Harbour, connected to the city centre with a wide boulevard lined with major commercial development; the completion of the Eastern Bay Link to provide an east-west

connection across south Cardiff and into the city centre; and extensive investment in landscape and public art to create a new public realm. An early intervention by CBDC was the placing of a key section of the link in a one kilometre tunnel from the science centre for children, Techniquest, to beyond Bute Avenue, a very expensive attempt to ensure strong connections between Mount Stuart Square and the waterfront.

Because of the property recession in the early 1990s, the regeneration of Cardiff Bay started slowly, and many investments required significant public subsidy. A development agreement was made with Associated British Ports and its property subsidiary, Grosvenor Waterside, to develop its 65 hectares on Roath Basin and the Ferry Road peninsula. The first commercial developments in the Bay were office buildings on their land - Crickhowell House now the National Assembly - and the striking NCM Building.

The Bay's 'unique selling point' was the vision of "a major maritime city" on a freshwater lake

Grosvenor Waterside is the property developer of Associated British Ports here in Cardiff. Since 1991 – after the Cardiff Bay Development Corporation provided the infrastructure of roads, sewage and communications – we have had the task of encouraging private property development. We have spent £63 million on what you see around you today. Of that, £6 million came from the government, a leverage of ten-to-one of private money. Take Atlantic Wharf – 12-screen cinema, restaurants, 24-lane bowling alley and parking for 1,000 cars. It was sold for £30 million to British Airways' pension fund before the foundations were down.
They knew, as we did, it would be a success.

ALAN DAVIES
EXECUTIVE DIRECTOR, GROSVENOR WATERSIDE

In 1997 five office buildings were completed around Scott Harbour. Also significant in employment terms were the upgrading of the Ocean Park Industrial Estate, and the attraction in 1994 of Nippon Electric Glass to the estate, employing 600 people.

The first major leisure investments in the 'arc of entertainment' were instant successes – Techniquest and Harry Ramsden's fish and chip restaurant. The Atlantic Wharf Multiplex cinema, bowling alley, restaurant and nightclub complex followed. The five star St David's Hotel was opened in 1999, anchoring the western end of the arc of entertainment, while the (now closed) Sports Café and Mermaid Quay - a shopping, restaurant and café bar complex - came in 1999, reinforcing visitor attractions at the heart of the Inner Harbour. The Welsh Industrial and Maritime Museum was closed by CBDC and relocated to Swansea Marina to allow the development of Roald Dahl Plass, a ceremonial and outdoor event space to front the new Wales Millennium Centre. To the east two diminutive but important attractions were the re-erected Norwegian Church and the futuristic tube of CBDC's Visitor Centre. So the ambitions for an 'arc of entertainment' around the Inner Harbour were realised, and by 2003 the area was receiving some five million visitors annually.

When the property market improved in the mid 1990s, it was clear that residential development was going to be the major driver of development in the Bay. Atlantic Wharf was built with a mixture of townhouses and apartment schemes, as was Windsor Quay on the west bank of the Taff. Adventurer's Quay occupied a key site on Roath Basin, and like Century Wharf on the east bank of the Taff, adopted a "gated community" approach. CBDC agreed to provide 840 units of social housing on various sites while setting itself a 25 per cent affordable target. By the early 2000s housing development was proceeding apace all across the Bay and as far west as the banks of the River Ely, and more medium-rise towers were being

built, raising the densities and capturing the views. Housing on Lloyd George Avenue benefited from the inputs of renowned architect Richard Reid as CBDC sought to upgrade the standard of design. This more interventionist approach was not maintained, though Barratt's Sovereign Quay project won national design awards.

A major element of the regeneration strategy was the Secretary of State for Wales' commitment to "the highest standards of design and quality in all types of investment". An experienced design and architecture review panel was established to review the design of each project, publishing its 'Policies for Urban Quality', and producing detailed area development briefs with design guidelines for seven areas of the Bay. These did achieve some increase in design quality, but success was limited by developers' reluctance to depart from single-use, freestanding buildings set in extensive car parking, and defensive attitudes to the street and passers-by. Nonetheless, the Corporation did deliver an exceptional level of architectural patronage throughout the Bay on individual buildings, spaces, landscapes and pieces of infrastructure. Architectural critics remember the failure to build Zaha Hadid's competition winning

A notable design success was public art.
Cardiff Bay was the first locality in the UK
to commission a Public Art Strategy

design for the new opera house. But the design failings of the Bay are not primarily ones of architectural imagination, but rather those of urban design, and it is the lack of coherent pieces of townscape, enclosed streets and distinct neighbourhoods that most disturb visitors to the Bay. Rectifying this will be a major task for the Council planners over the next decade.

A notable design success was public art. Cardiff Bay was the first locality in the UK to commission a public art strategy and a "per cent for art" policy was implemented by the Cardiff Bay Arts Trust, producing some remarkable, much-loved pieces like John Gingell's transformation of an electricity sub station, and the Merchant Seafarers' War Memorial at the Pierhead by Brian Fell.

There were 16 sewage outlets pouring into the Bay, and when the tide went out and left the mudflat showing, the whole place reeked, especially in the summer. Two-hundred yards away was a primary school and people living down here, a lot of them black. So, no one north of the tracks gave a damn. There weren't any 'good ol' days' in Tiger Bay. The incidence of TB down here was the highest in the country. Those who talk about how wonderful it was just don't know. I don't remember anything good about the past.

LORD JACK BROOKS
FORMER LEADER, SOUTH GLAMORGAN COUNCIL

The biggest problem was how to provide a clear, direct link between the Bay and the city centre that could be utilised by pedestrians, cyclists and public transport. High ambitions were set out by retaining one of Europe's leading architects, David Mackay of the Barcelona practice of MBM, to design a new 'Ramblas' to link the city centre to the Oval Basin. However, the future of the railway and its Bute Street embankment were never resolved, and arguments for a great public boulevard for promenading down to the Bay were always dubious given local weather, and the high housing densities that would be necessary to make the boulevard work. Eventually in 1999 a scheme was funded through a £128 million Private Finance Initiative with construction companies and developers. A new public open space, Callaghan Square, was built at the northern end as the focus of an office area, and the east side of the boulevard was lined with four-storey apartments. Even this solution was subverted by the failure of the owners of the rail track to resolve the future of their route to the Bay. A regular bus link to the Bay has now been provided, but until the tract of land between Lloyd George Avenue and Bute Street is developed with a mix of medium density private and social housing, there will be no social link between the Bay communities and the city centre.

Baltimore was interesting to us because its old dock area is almost exactly the same size as Cardiff's. In a remarkably short period of time, Baltimore had managed to create the Inner Harbour, swanky hotels and restaurants, and linked the old city with its seafront. It was all happening there and it was a great success. Yes, Baltimore became our inspiration.

LORD CRICKHOWELL
FORMER SECRETARY OF STATE FOR WALES

An overall evaluation of the achievements of CBDC has to take into account the difficult national economic climate during much of its existence, and the delays and setbacks occasioned by legislative and certain development controversies. A National Audit local and central government taxes, and there were assets of £323 million in terms of property, open spaces and the Barrage. A key measure of economic success for development corporations is the so-called 'gearing ratio' of public and private investment.

The Corporation made efforts to address unemployment and the socially disadvantaged in Cardiff Bay, securing some 1,500 jobs for residents

Office report in 2001 showed that while the Corporation had fallen short of its original targets, it nevertheless was on course to exceed most of them in the foreseeable future. Forty-one per cent of the cost of the regeneration of Cardiff Bay was spent on the Barrage as well as the continuing costs of commissioning and maintaining the freshwater lake. Against these, the Audit Office concluded the Bay was returning £170 million annually to the public purse in

For the Bay project, the amount spent from the public purse steadily declined in relation to private investment.

The Corporation made efforts to address unemployment and the socially disadvantaged in Cardiff Bay, securing some 1,500 jobs for residents and 268 of its trainees. It gave grants of £3.3 million to training schemes and £2.8 million to community development, and spent over £6 million on housing,

primary schools and landscape improvements. But while it was set the objective "to reflect the hopes and aspirations of the communities in the area", its political targets were money invested, jobs created, housing units and infrastructure built. For all its activity it had a minor impact upon the level and concentration of social disadvantage in the area.

> Tiger Bay society is the oldest continuous multi-ethnic community in Britain, and was never a black community. From the beginning it was always a multi-racial and intra-cultural community. In Tiger Bay there were not all-black schools or institutions. When community members point homeward to the lands of their ancestral forefathers, they point to Egypt, Yemen, Arabia, Somaliland, Sierra Leone, Nigeria, Malta, Cape Verde, Spain and the islands of the Caribbean. By the 1950s Tiger Bay was a nation unto itself.
>
> **THE TIGER BAY STORY**
> NEIL M.C. SINCLAIR
> (BUTETOWN HISTORY & ARTS CENTRE, 1993)

The ambitions for Cardiff that were evident in the regeneration plans for the Bay began to be translated into explicit Euro-Capital

agendas at both County and City Council levels. The City Council's views were less 'boosterist' than those of the County, recognising the city region's economic under-performance. South Glamorgan County Council published its 'Towards 2002' vision statement in 1994 which emphasised the importance of preserving and enhancing the city's quality of life and sharing prosperity amongst its citizens. The 1990 Local Plan contrasted buoyant service growth and a thriving city centre with concentrations of social disadvantage in inner city wards. The early 1990s saw improvements to the city centre in modest ways through conservation and pedestrian improvements, of which the Mill Lane Café Quarter was one of the most successful.

> We might attract the wrong sort of attention and wrong type of visitors if we rely only on major sports and mass entertainment. We might succeed only in reinforcing the stereotypes of Wales – rugby and a singsong. To succeed and enhance perceptions of the city we need a festival atmosphere which is far more attractive to a far wider audience. Let's concentrate on quality – not quantity – both of visitors and attractions.
>
> **BOB CROYDON**
> PARTNER, KING STURGE PROPERTY, CARDIFF

The County had already signalled its 'Euro-capital city' aspirations, rescuing the Welsh Rugby Union's bid to stage the 1999 Rugby World Cup, obtaining a grant of £46 million from the Millennium Commission for the 72,000-seat Millennium Stadium, and seizing the opportunity to market the city on a world stage. The staging of the European Summit in Cardiff in 1998 was an unexpected but welcome windfall putting Cardiff firmly on the European stage, and gave the city experience of managing major events in partnership with business and other agencies. Hotel development in particular was boosted as the city geared up for these events. An action plan was developed to deliver improvements to Central Station and Central Square. A new walkway alongside the River Taff was constructed to provide pedestrian access to the stadium, and Millennium Plaza was created where the Empire Pool had been. The happy accident of the redevelopment of Wembley in London boosted the Stadium's global success and dramatically raised the profile of Cardiff as an international visitor destination.

The County had already signalled its 'Euro-capital city' aspirations, rescuing the Welsh Rugby Union's bid to stage the 1999 Rugby World Cup

LLEWELYN
EIN LLYW OLAF
LLEWELYN
THE LAST PRINCE
DIED 1282
HENRY PEGRAM A.R.A.
SCULPTOR

The County had already signalled its 'Euro-capital city' aspirations, rescuing the Welsh Rugby Union's bid to stage the 1999 Rugby World Cup.

LLEWELYN
EIN LLYW OLAF
LLEWELYN
THE LAST PRINCE
DIED 1282

HENRY PEGRAM A·R·A
SCULPTOR

Amidst these major successes there was one pressing challenge. It had always been assumed the new Welsh Assembly would move into City Hall, retaining proximity to the civil servants, reinforcing the civic centre, and reusing one of the city's great architectural assets. But the Assembly balked at the £24 million price tag placed on it by the Council, which had to re-house a large number of employees and satisfy auditors that they had achieved a fair price for the ratepayers of Cardiff. The competition that ensued between Cardiff and Swansea, won by Cardiff with a site in the Bay, alienated some sections of opinion across Wales. The city was seen as anti-Assembly and garnering too much public resource despite evidence that it subsidises other parts of Wales. Fortunately the new Assembly building in the Bay, designed by one of the world's foremost architectural consultancies, the Richard Rogers Partnership, is superb - and at a tenth of the cost of the Scottish Assembly.

> For most of the Welsh population Cardiff remains a centre for permanent suspicion. It is regarded as too English, too flash, too large and far too anti-Welsh for many. Half of its population still think they live in the West Country. The rest don't care. Nevertheless, the excitement of being in one of the newest of European capitals hangs light in the air. All you have to do is to stand in the middle of Queen Street and look at the place. Something is going on – and going on at a considerable rate. But we're not quite sure what it is, are we, Mrs. Jones?
>
> **PETER FINCH**
> REAL CARDIFF (SEREN, 2004)

To drive forward the "truly international city centre" agenda an initiative was launched in 1996 seeking to establish the active collaboration of the key private sector interests in a partnership with the Council and the Chamber of Commerce. Six priority areas were identified including transport, office development, housing, tourism, environment and the development of the "24 hour city". Regular monitoring of pedestrian flows, visitor profiles and opinions were introduced to underpin town centre management, and an annual City Centre Strategy document was developed. The Council secured developer contributions to pay for improvements to the Friary, the pedestrianisation of Caroline Street and the repaving of Queen Street.

A City Centre Living Strategy was introduced to encourage affordable housing developments, but over the last few years major private house builders have woken up to the potential of city

centre living. The conversion of the first 1960s office block to residential - The Aspect at the end of Queen Street - and the city's first new purpose-built high rise apartments, Landmark Place on Churchill Way, have been followed by five high rise schemes along the main railway line. These projects signal a huge change of scale and building height in the city, and may highlight a need for a policy to guide the location and form of tall buildings in Cardiff.

The proposed St David's 2 development will cover over16 hectares, include over 100 new stores, expand the city centre retail offer by 28 per cent, and will employ 4,000 people

A major expansion of city centre shopping had been a major objective in Cardiff for over a decade, particularly the attraction of another prestige department store. By early 2003 the Council was negotiating with Land Securities, the owners of the St David's Centre and the parent company of Ravenseft, about a major retail investment south of St David's Centre, and an outline planning permission was granted later that year for the St David's 2 development.

The proposed St David's 2 development will cover over 16 hectares, include over 100 new stores, expand the city centre retail offer by 28 per cent, and will employ 4,000 people. It will include significant office, hotel and residential uses, as well as an additional 1,800 car parking places. The new centre will propel Cardiff up the national retail hierarchy in the UK, expanding its regular retail catchment to include almost half of Wales. There is still some refining of the proposals to be done to ensure the project revitalises the south east corner of the city centre. The new shopping will inevitably increase traffic congestion and car use within the city, require significant reworking and reorganisation of bus services, parking and the road network, but will revitalise The Hayes and include a new public library for Cardiff.

Three other mega projects provide markers of a new scale of development in the southern part of the city. The most ambitious is the International Sports Village on the Ferry Road peninsula, which is estimated to attract 4.5 million visitors, create 3,500 jobs on site, and attract an annual spend of over £200 million when it is complete. The proposals include a 50 - metre swimming pool, a leisure pool, an arena and ice rink with 4,000 seats, a snow-box for winter sports, and a hotel. But what seems likely to re-shape the whole project is the inclusion of an international resort casino taking advantage of the relaxation of UK gambling laws.

The second mega project is the proposed redevelopment of Ninian Park and replacement of Leckwith Stadium with a new stadium for Cardiff City Football Club. A 40,000 square metre retail and leisure park with a large supermarket, DIY store and 15 bulky goods warehouses are being built to help cover a percentage of the total development costs. Significant community benefits have been negotiated as part of the development.

The third mega project is a major Welsh Development Agency urban regeneration initiative on a redundant former dockland site to provide a mix of commercial and residential development on the eastern shore of Cardiff Bay. The commercial proposal is for a Life Sciences Business Cluster, which will include a Technium and business incubation centre, primarily for small enterprises in the Life Sciences sector. The centre will benefit from on-site support facilities and a dedicated Incubation Manager. There will also be opportunities within the overall commercial development of 1 million square feet for enterprises from local, regional and inward investment to occupy quality buildings, thereby assisting in the development of the economy of Cardiff and providing a range of job opportunities in the knowledge-based sectors. In addition, approximately 1,000 residential units will be developed on attractive waterside sites overlooking the inner harbour.

Two of these three projects emphasise the importance of commercial leisure fused with retail as a generator of investment and employment, and all three epitomise the changing economic base and pattern of employment in the city.

Fortunately, the planners' 1964 vision of a massive city centre driven northwards by high rise office development and criss-crossed by urban motorways has not been realised. Instead, modest commercial and strong residential growth southwards has created an enlarged but looser city centre, dispersing some key cultural and administrative functions to Cardiff Bay, and creating new inner city residential areas. "A truly superlative European capital city", and the "most exciting waterfront in Europe" remain long term aspirations, but notwithstanding the marketing, the city centre now boasts a range of facilities and amenities that very few cities of its size possess.

The lower productivity of the Welsh economy, the cyclical nature of the property market which often reaches Wales as it weakens nationally, the drawing off of over 45 per cent of Cardiff's business rates to the rest of Wales, and 30 years of government restraint

on local taxation and public expenditure, have to some extent restricted the aspirations both of Cardiff and the Council. Practically the only way the city can generate significant funds for investment in infrastructure and new and improved public facilities is to enter into public-private partnerships where commercial realities dictate what is achievable. So, the new St David's 2 Shopping Centre will finance city centre pedestrianisation improvements, while the International Sports Village will deliver a new swimming pool, albeit under private ownership and management. As the city faces continued financial pressures it has to turn its attention to other ways of raising funds to fulfil its European capital ambitions, as evidenced by its ambitious public-private partnership proposals for the provision of transport.

> We do not just want Cardiff to be the capital of Wales. We want it to be the capital for Wales. The city can play a major role in driving forward the economic, social and cultural development of Wales, sharing its wealth and its facilities with the nation at large.
>
> **RUSSELL GOODWAY**
> FORMER LEADER, CARDIFF COUNTY COUNCIL

The immediate future of the city centre is exciting. The completion of the St David's 2 Shopping Centre in 2008 will provide a massive economic boost to the city centre and create a north-south retail axis to rival Queen Street. It will reinforce the viability of all the Victorian arcades, and encourage the refurbishment, if not the redevelopment of the Cardiff International Arena, and revitalise the south east of the city centre.

High-rise residential redevelopment will proceed along the north side of the railway, where several towers are currently being mooted in addition to the Altolusso development on the site of the former New College School, and the transformation of former Council offices on Greyfriars Road to residential and hotel uses is nearly complete. Major changes are likely to the Newport Road office area which is diversifying to hotel and university uses, while office developers seek new sites in old industrial area such as the top of Dumballs Road. Callaghan Square waits for more tenants to make new buildings viable. Perhaps a wider range of new residents and tighter local controls on licensing will help resist the expansion of the 'Binge Culture' and support a broader range of investment in catering and entertainment that can improve some of the city's

more attractive backwaters like Westgate and Womanby Streets. Perhaps entrepreneurial landowners will extend the Castle Arcade westwards, and link Hills Street east to Churchill Way and Queen Street Station to continue Cardiff's tradition of intricate east-west links across the centre.

> By any standards Cardiff has good rail services, particularly to London. The journey time is one hour 55 minutes and there is half hourly frequency during the working day. In those terms it is one of the best in Europe.
>
> **THE WALES TRANSPORT RESEARCH CENTRE**
> UNIVERSITY OF GLAMORGAN

Traffic and public transportation circulation will also change significantly in the wake of St David's 2. There are plans to move the bus station to the north east of the station to allow the commercial redevelopment of Central Square. The Chamber of Commerce suggest a convention centre here, but the Council would prefer to see this located adjacent to the Stadium. New transport plans would mean no disruption of bus routes when the Millennium Stadium is in use, would allow the removal of private cars from St Mary's Street, and might even lead to the creation of a true civic space between the civic centre and Greyfriar's Road, a long overdue if expensive amenity, but a characteristic of all other European capitals. The development of the futuristic automated urban transport system, known as ULTRA, is favoured by some as a means of connecting transport nodes and attractions, and would certainly give the city a high profile in the transport field.

The final set of changes depend upon the City's cultural budget, and whether it can fund those missing pieces of the "European Capital" jigsaw – a Cardiff museum, a modern art gallery, a national theatre, a centrally located arts centre, a quality venue for large pop concerts. Bute Park and Sophia Gardens would benefit from a regeneration plan to create facilities that will attract visitors year round and complement the park landscape, connecting it properly into the heart of the city. Plans to provide a water bus link to the Bay have been put in place and the Waterbus operates daily giving visitors to Cardiff's waterfront a unique view of Cardiff from the water. The Waterbus sails daily between Penarth, Cardiff Bay and the city centre.

In the Bay the opening of the 'flagship' Wales Millennium Centre and the National Assembly Buildings are breathing new life into existing businesses in the Arc of Entertainment, and increasing interest in commercial office building in the immediate vicinity.

> Today we hand over this wonderful building to the people of Wales, to the performers of the world and to our audiences and visitors from across the four corners of the globe. It is an historic moment and a very proud moment for all involved.
>
> **SIR DAVID ROWE-BEDDOE**
> CHAIRMAN, WALES MILLENNIUM CENTRE

Much will depend upon the completion of the Peripheral Distributor Road to the east to provide improved access to the Bay, and to spur redevelopment of the industrial and storage areas between Roath Basin and Wentloog. Nonetheless the Bay's future seems largely residential, though the International Sports Village entertainment complex will provide a second major focus of entertainment.

The major challenge in the Bay will be to improve its accessibility and its environmental coherence, to better integrate the diverse residential areas and give them the services and amenities they need. Foremost among the priorities is the reintegration of the Butetown estate - physically, economically and socially - into the Bay community. Closely related is the need to improve the connection between the Bay and the city centre by making Lloyd George Avenue a real boulevard. The reduction of reliance on the car for the journey to work in the Bay is an absolute priority. Reliable direct links to the railway stations and the city centre, and the full integration of public transport are an absolute priority.

Much remains to be done on a smaller scale to encourage small pieces of infill development and refurbishment, new pedestrian and landscape links, and to connect existing housing schemes with civilised and safe streets into a coherent set of neighbourhoods. On the larger scale there is a need for an ambitious landscape and ecology plan for the Bay and the river valleys.

The city's promoting growth strategy certainly needs to give more attention to the quality of development, as was recognised in its bid for the City of Culture 2008. Two priorities suggest themselves. First, more attention needs to be paid to highway design, with more consistent traffic calming, particularly in the Bay, and greater attention to pedestrian and cyclist needs. Repaving and refurnishing, public art and landscape all need to reach European provincial city standards. Second, there is a need to raise the quality of architecture and urban design in the city. There are allusions to this in recent Council reports and promises of new design guidance. A routine insistence on design quality is characteristic of most major north European cities, not just the superlative ones.

Some see this as the counsel of perfection, as unachievable in the current economic climate. They point quite rightly to the massive improvements made to the city centre and the Bay since the mid 1970s, to Cardiff's present high ranking in the UK in terms of retail vitality, to high levels of visitor satisfaction, and to the increasing diversification of the city centre offer. But as the city places increasing emphasis on attracting affluent international tourists

The International Sports Village entertainment complex will provide a second major focus of entertainment

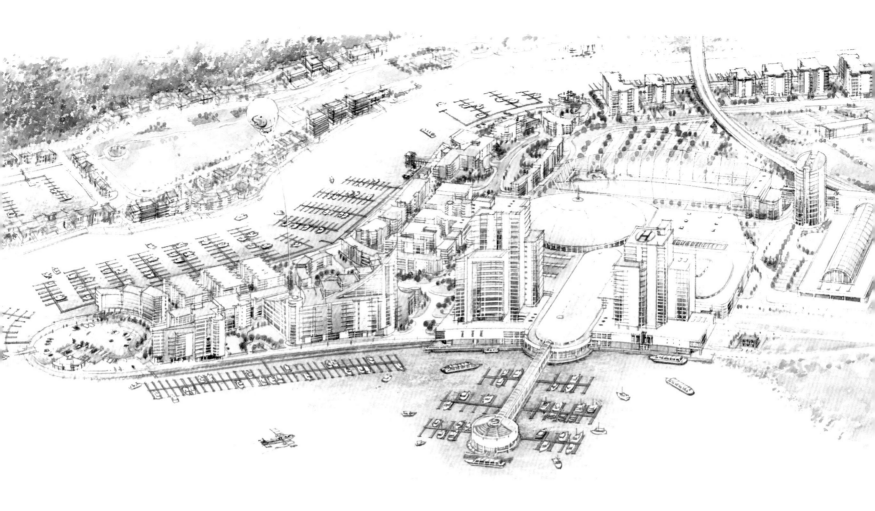

through cruise ship terminals, casinos and conventions, so the quality of the city's environment, its streets and townscape and its 'local distinctiveness' must increase to retain such business. And all the residents of Cardiff and Wales must be able to share fully in the enjoyment of these essentially public assets, as well as benefit from the increased employment and prosperity it will bring.

> Cardiff is undergoing a period of exciting change which will make the city even more dynamic. It is of great importance that Cardiff is seen on a world stage to cement and build on the international relationships that have already been forged.
>
> **RODNEY BERMAN**
> LEADER OF CARDIFF COUNCIL

Prof Mike Edmunds
Head of the School of Astronomy and Physics, Cardiff University dressed as Sir Isaac Newton for one of his periodic one-man shows about science

"

Science is alive and well and living in Cardiff. Much of the work of scientists here is of national and international importance. Here in Physics, for example, we construct instruments that will go on satellites and in telescopes. I have seen this university grow and get better over the 30 years I have been here. The city itself has changed beyond all recognition, and is a wonderful place to live and work.

For scientists and science students, institutions such as Techniquest demonstrate Cardiff's commitment to helping to popularise science and technology. That's exactly why I occasionally dress as Newton or Einstein and do my little one-man play. I want to show that scientists are people, not eccentrics in white coats in laboratories. This demystifies science. People can be very afraid of science and not realise it is a human activity. If I can give them some glimpse into the lives of scientists they have heard about, perhaps I can interest them in science itself. We have to make political, social and cultural decisions based on science and technology. The more people understand about the processes of science, the more intelligent those decisions will be. "

"

I graduated in geography and then did a Masters in pollution and environmental control. I joined the Cardiff Harbour Authority when it was established in 2000. Many of us working here in the Environment Team have the same academic background.

By keeping the water quality of Cardiff Bay pristine, it means that people can come and enjoy the area for watersports. As to development around the Bay, both residential and commercial, we liaise with developers to ensure minimal environmental impact.

We like to think of ourselves as pioneers. There is no other place in the UK that has a 200 hectare man-made freshwater lake. It has attracted a lot of scientific interest because of the issues we have to face. The Bay is the most intensively monitored body of water in Europe. We monitor it '24/7' with a dedicated team. There is no other waterfront development with so much investment and resources set aside to keep it as near-perfect as we can get it.

All this work is due to the Act of Parliament that made the Cardiff Bay Barrage possible and it sets very strict standards. In dissolved oxygen levels for example, there is a lot of global interest about the stringent standard we have to maintain. This is being written about in scientific journals and it's pretty exciting for scientists like us who work here.

The Barrage was controversial in some respects, and that means there is still a lot of interest in our operations. The natural environment is very important to us and the creation of the Cardiff Bay Wetlands Reserve is a good example of our commitment. We have now recorded over 100 species of bird and 20 species of fish here. We are trying to create an eco-system here that balances the needs of the environment and the needs of people. We are happy with the results so far.

"

Annie Middleton

Environment
Officer – Cardiff
Harbour
Authority

Housing and Community Regeneration
Chapter 4

Adapted from text by Bob Smith & Alan Hooper

It's a capital the Welsh can be proud of. The first city of Wales is on a high…

Lonely Planet Guide, Wales

Chester Street, Grangetown, consists of rows of identical terraced houses. They were built in the late 19th Century for workers of the Great Western Railway. All but one of the 20 or so houses that line the street were sold to the railwaymen. Number 9 was purchased by Emmett Hughes, a bricklayer who helped build the terraces, including his own 'two-up-and-two-down' house. He paid £8 and 10 shillings. Today it is valued at £145,000.

A century later, Grangetown and several other Cardiff neighbourhoods have their own 'Chester Street', repeated in one symmetrical square after another. All were Victorian versions of cheap, mass-produced housing. And, they differ very little from the kind of residential property of that period found in countless British cities.

A home must satisfy two paradoxical claims. It must be an efficient machine through which the family income can be spent to best advantage, but it must also be a place to which the family returns with relief and satisfaction – which will meet their needs as individuals, as opposed to their duties and enjoyment as citizens, neighbours, workers and children.

ELIZABETH DENBY
BRITAIN'S FIRST WOMAN HOUSING CONSULTANT,
(PICTURE POST, 1941)

The quantity and quality of housing in any community is the product of an array of factors – taste, price, scarcity, land prices and availability, government policy, and the state of the economy. Where they are located, how many occupy a certain space, their style – are also the product of planning – that often contentious process of balancing the community's social, housing and commercial needs with environmental and aesthetic concerns. What is built in weeks or months communities must live with for decades, even centuries. Concrete, mortar, bricks and steel are lasting, and the way they are placed and shaped can have a dramatic impact on people, even their health and well-being.

When Cardiff first developed as a coal metropolis between 1870 and 1914, the relationship between its built environment and its population was largely determined by links between employment and the housing market, and of course, who owned the land. Prior to the First World War most families rented, and it is only in the last 80 years that this has been overtaken by private home ownership and rented homes offered by the Council and housing associations. Advances in transportation, and in particular private car ownership, had a major impact upon the shape of Cardiff.

What is left of the former coal metropolis is the inner area of Cardiff, typified by streets like Chester Street in Grangetown. Over the past 30 years especially, that shape has begun to change as the city has expanded not only in population but also spatially and functionally. Home ownership, both within inner areas and in the

Cardiff's population increase in the 19th Century was phenomenal. In 1801 it had just over 1,000 inhabitants

suburbs, together with the post-second World War growth in Council housing development in areas such as Ely, Llanrumney and Butetown – all left their imprint on Cardiff, making it the city it is today. At the same time, large swathes of late Victorian and Edwardian housing remain, though its quality is variable. In some instances, the city's older housing stock has adapted well to the changing needs of Cardiff's people. Housing originally built for families is now increasingly used to accommodate the city's growing number of single person households of all ages and circumstances, and a growing student population.

> I knew all about Elin Owen next-door, and her husband, Gruffydd Owen the sailor; when I heard laughter through the window, I knew for certain who was there; when a child passed by on the road, I could tell the history of its father and mother and grandparents... When I was a child I could describe the mantelpiece of almost every house in the whole neighbourhood.
>
> **EXILE IN CARDIFF**
> W.J.RUFFED

In recent years the transformation of housing in Cardiff has been triggered by the regeneration of Cardiff Bay. With the establishment of the Cardiff Bay Development Corporation in late 1986 came new homes and apartments, and opportunities for new

private and social housing. The Council's own strategies have reinforced moves to attract people to live in the Bay and now, in the city centre itself, with developments at Atlantic Wharf, Windsor Quay, Lloyd George Avenue and Sovereign Quay providing a mix of new and attractive types of housing. At the same time that these new residential developments helped to meet Cardiff's housing needs and demands, contributing to the regeneration of the city, they also threw up a range of challenges which still need to be addressed.

> Over the river bridge we went before a soul was stirring, and into the heart of the town. There in Custom House Street, which is Cardiff's Covent Garden, I held the pony while the woman chaffered over boxes of kippers and crates of oranges, sacks of potatoes - all the ingredients of her picturesque calling. Dead though the city might be elsewhere, Custom House Street was wide awake, full of champing horses, and rattling harnesses, and shouting men; and the pavements exhaled into the still frosty air their unforgettable smell of trodden vegetables...
>
> **HOWARD SPRING**
> THE ERRAND BOY, 1939

Cardiff's population increase in the 19th Century was phenomenal. In 1801 it had just over 1,000 inhabitants. This rose to over 18,000 by the middle of the century, and to 182,000 by 1911, when the export of coal was at its height. By the time of the 1971 Census, Cardiff's population was almost 280,000. Ten years later the city's population was recorded as having fallen slightly. Today the official population exceeds 315,000. During the 1990s, over 12,000 new

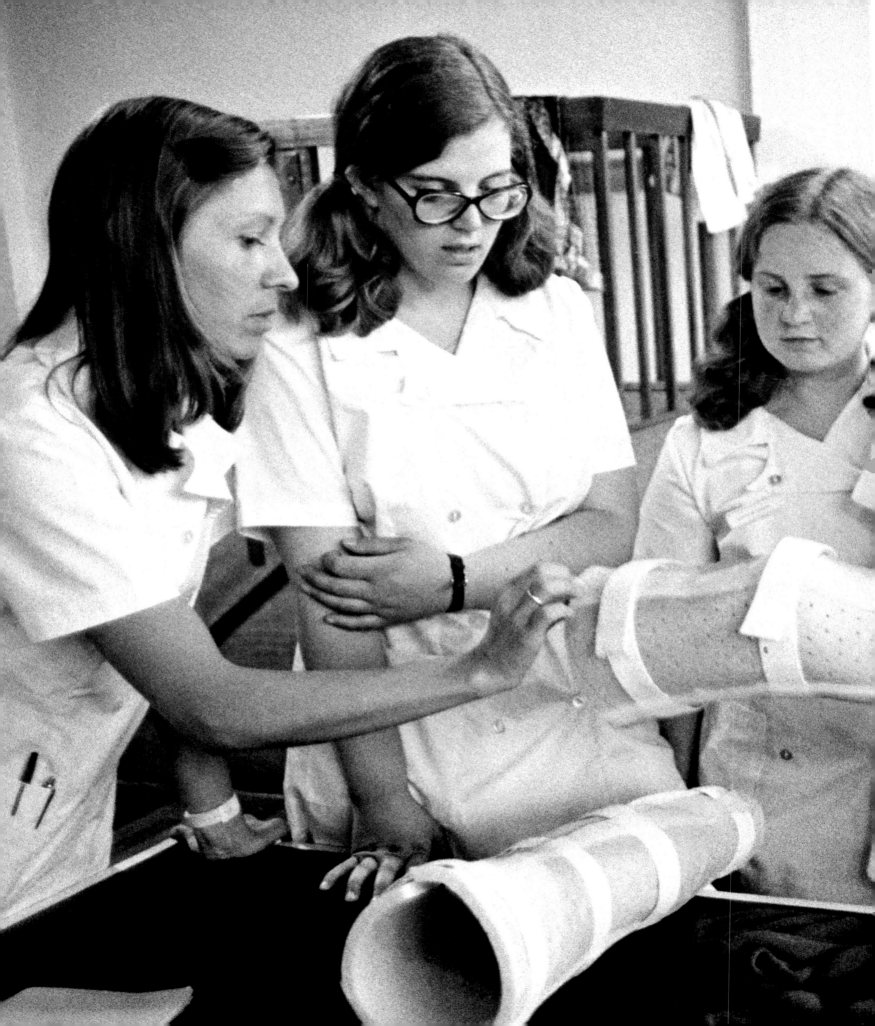

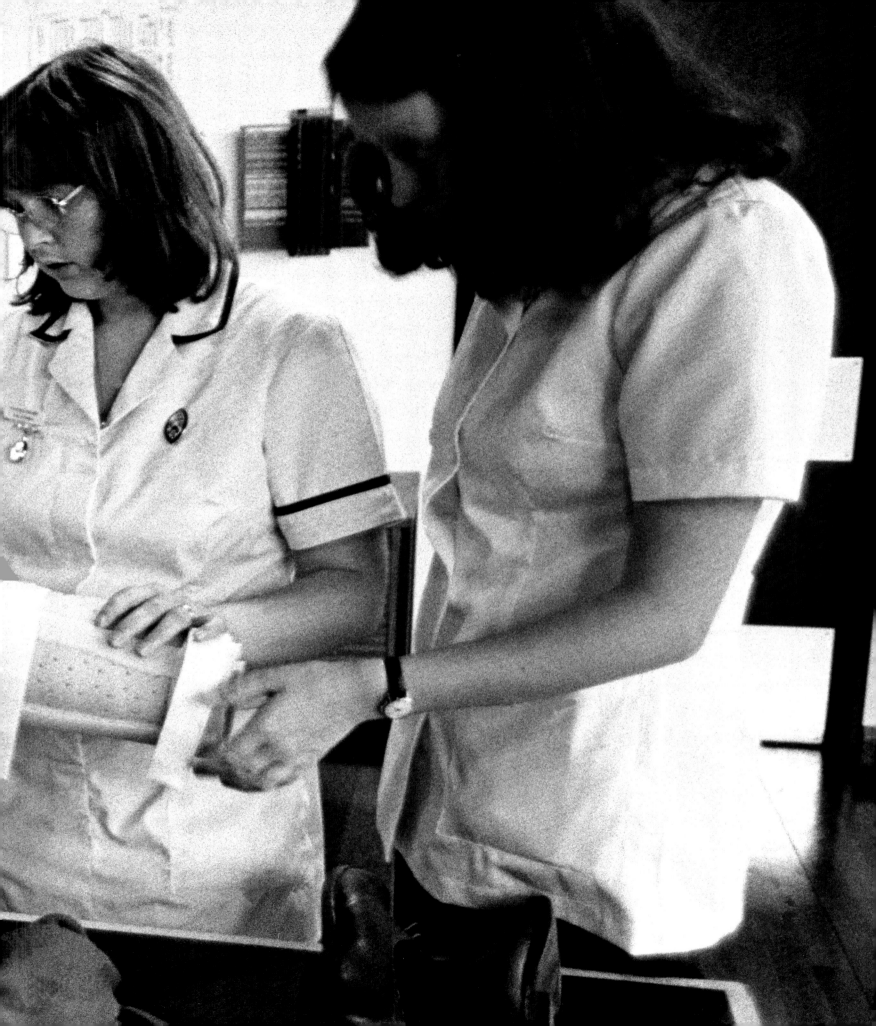

dwellings were built in Cardiff, almost 30,000 additional jobs created and over 10,000 more full-time places made available in higher education.

Cardiff has a long history of diversity and multiculturalism. Its population includes groups originating from the Caribbean, Somalia, India, Pakistan, Bangladesh and other parts of South East Asia. The 2001 Census recorded an ethnic minority population in Cardiff of nearly eight and a half per cent – but many think that is an underestimate. Whatever the figure, over half of all of Wales' non-white population live in Cardiff, the majority concentrated in Butetown, Riverside, Grangetown, Adamsdown, Cathays and Plasnewydd.

Cardiff experienced considerable social regeneration over the last 25 years, and this has been underpinned by a concerted drive to improve educational outcomes for the city's school pupils. Successful schools are a key factor in any society and education is crucial for the success of a city. It has been the aim of successive Council's to develop Cardiff as a city of educational excellence and to develop an education system that creates opportunities and enables individuals to achieve their full potential.

The future of education in Cardiff rests on taking the service forward into the 21st Century and considerable progress has been made in terms of pupils' achievements. But there is always room for improvement. The Council now faces the challenge of dealing with falling pupil numbers, surplus school places and maintaining quality school buildings and must ensure that schools work closely together, sharing resources, buildings and staff to meet the needs of children and wider communities.

Unemployment is relatively low in Cardiff, but there are areas where three quarters of households are dependent upon means-tested benefits, and where more than one in four children live in homes which get some form of income support. Moreover, there are parts of the city where poor health, diet and relatively high levels of smoking and alcohol consumption are blamed for higher early mortality rates. Cardiff's plans for improving the health and well-being of its citizens have been set out in a Health, Social Care and Well-Being Strategy, which is designed to tackle the causes of ill-health, reduce health inequalities and promote higher quality health and social care services for residents. A healthier city, with high levels of service provision, is seen as prerequisites for continued progress.

Cardiff has a long history of diversity and multiculturalism. Its population includes groups originating from the Caribbean, Somalia, India, Pakistan, Bangladesh and other parts of South East Asia

This progress has been helped by several key developments that have greatly improved Cardiff's social infrastructure. A milestone in the development of health care provision in Cardiff was the opening by the Queen in November 1971 of the University Hospital of Wales, or Heath Hospital, and the key to Wales' first children's hospital was handed over to the Cardiff and Vale NHS Trust on St David's Day 2005, marking its official opening as a working hospital.

Although the numbers of those aged 85 and over continues to increase, Cardiff doesn't have a particularly large elderly population, especially compared to other parts of Wales. But the city is struggling to provide adequate care and support. The closure of long stay geriatric provision in the 1980s, with care for the elderly replaced by private residential and nursing homes, has led to a more mixed provision of services. However, with higher care standards leading to rising costs, some of these establishments are no longer economically viable and the Council, together with other partner organisations, are having to look at developing different models of providing accommodation with appropriate levels of care and support for the elderly. Tackling these issues for other vulnerable and disadvantaged groups will not only contribute to improved health and well-being but also the wider regeneration agenda.

Successful community regeneration is also dependent on developing effective strategies to tackle crime, the fear of crime, substance misuse and anti-social behaviour. The Cardiff Community Safety Partnership brings together the Council, Police, Fire Service, Heath Service, Probation Service, the Local Criminal Justice Board and other agencies to tackle these problems within Cardiff. It seeks to engage with local communities through local Elected Members, community groups, road shows and school liaison. The Partnership also recognises the value of consulting with the residents of Cardiff, including groups of interest, to keep up-to-date with their concerns and needs and to give them the

opportunity to get involved in local decision making. Efforts are also made to raise awareness of community safety initiatives through a variety of media, including the local press, which gives the Partnership an opportunity to bring its work to the public's attention.

Second tier community based policing has also been welcomed in Cardiff. This comprises both Police Community Support Officers (PCSOs), who are employed and deployed by South Wales Police, and are recognisable to the public by their distinct uniform. In addition to these, some employees from various organisations, including the Council, who already have a role in enforcement, have been made 'Accredited Community Safety Officers'. This gives them additional enforcement powers, such as enabling them to issue fixed penalty notices.

In Cardiff, Anti Social Behaviour Orders (ASBOs) are used only as a last resort in addressing anti-social behaviour. The main emphasis is on developing closer partnerships, working to tackle some of the

underlying problems and focusing on challenging and diverting this type of behaviour.

Housing issues in any community raise a number of questions. First, how much housing should be provided, and where? Then, what quality is required? And finally, what balance should there be between private and social housing, and between housing to rent and housing for sale? Underlying each of these issues is the question of affordability. And like every village, town and city in Britain, this is one of Cardiff's most pressing issues.

Whereas the 19th Century expansion of the city was mainly in relatively well-built terraced housing, Cardiff's inter-war growth was influenced by the first private sector housing boom and the provision of Council housing estates. Typically, both took the form of ribbon development influenced by the English Garden City movement. In the private sector the most common dwelling was the semi-detached house, with terraced and semi-detached cottage style developments in the Council sector. Due to the comparatively small scale of Cardiff, the degree of segregation between private and social housing was relatively muted between the two world wars. However, in the post-Second World War period, with the significant growth in Council housing provision, clearer lines became evident.

Since the 1970s, private sector housing has continued to expand, whereas the Council sector has declined as a result of changes in legislation and the right to buy properties. In the private sector the development of detached houses is more common, although the

original low densities of 20-25 dwellings to the hectare have been increasingly squeezed by escalating land prices and the impact of planning policies. That also means a reduction in the size of the average house and its surrounding land. Still, the demand for such housing has fuelled continued suburban expansion, supported by rising household income and increasing car ownership. Where planning policies – such as the proposed green belt around the city – have impacted upon land availability, demand for housing has been exported beyond the city boundaries to areas such as Rhondda Cynon Taff, Caerphilly, Bridgend and Newport.

All of these elements combined add up to stress – pressure on land and housing, something that is happening in virtually every large city in the UK. Over time the city's main housing concerns have centred on questions of quality, including environmental quality, affordability, social exclusion and neighbourhood management issues such as tackling crime and anti-social behaviour. Only more recently have long-term strategic issues such as housing requirements, supply and land availability moved once again to the fore. Within the Council housing sector, national policy developments such as the right-to-buy have led to a mixing of tenure on estates, although its scale and impact varies across different neighbourhoods. Those residents remaining in the Council sector are increasingly concentrated amongst older, retired households and younger tenants, often dependent upon benefits and with relatively high support needs. Some of the older Council estates, erected between the wars, are experiencing high levels of disadvantage, anti-social behaviour and crime. In spite of the constraints, the Council has sought to combat these problems

Remember that our children and grandchildren
are going to do things that would stagger us

through programmes of community development and regeneration. In responding to the need for additional housing, the city has a two-pronged strategy. Suburban development is being promoted in areas such as St Mellons and Pontprennau. However, from the late 1980s onwards, greater emphasis was placed on "brownfield" development, particularly in the city centre and in Cardiff Bay.

Moreover, while initial attention focused upon attracting private sector housing into Cardiff Bay, one out of every four houses or apartments ended up as social housing. This was largely achieved through a combination of housing association and partnership schemes, supported by an increasing use of new planning legislation to secure affordable housing as part of the mix.

Overall, a significant proportion of the new housing provided in Cardiff Bay are apartments, which has helped to restore a balance of need for this type of accommodation within the city. Many of the schemes are high density, and include gated communities where public access is denied. The general housing layout and built form evident in Cardiff Bay is in marked contrast to elsewhere in the city, and initial research suggests that private housing here serves different demographic and socio-economic groups from that of the rest of the city. Nevertheless, the issue of housing affordability remains a problem within Cardiff Bay, with escalating land and property prices excluding lower income households. Concern has also been expressed at the comparative failure to link the residential development in Cardiff Bay to the older existing heartland communities of south Cardiff.

> Make no little plans. They have no magic to stir men's blood and probably themselves will not be realised. Make big plans; aim high in hope and work, remembering that a noble, logical diagram once recorded will never die, but long after we are gone will be a living thing, asserting itself with ever-growing insistency. Remember that our children and grandchildren are going to do things that would stagger us.
>
> **DANIEL BURNHAM**
> CHICAGO ARCHITECT, 1864-1912

In 1980 the total number of dwellings in Cardiff was over 100,000, of which nearly three-quarters were privately owned, mostly owner-occupied, but also properties owned by private landlords. Just under a quarter of the city's housing was owned and managed by the Council, with only two per cent provided by housing associations. Over 2,200 new homes were built in Cardiff between 1979 and 1980, of which more than 1,300 were provided either by the Council or by housing associations. In comparison, in April 2002 the estimated dwelling stock for Cardiff was over 129,000, with more than eight out of 10 privately owned and two-thirds of those owner-occupied. These figures illustrate not only the growth in Cardiff's housing stock, but also the continued rise in private housing ownership within the city – a trend seen across the UK over the last 25 years.

There has also been growth in privately rented properties in Cardiff, as in many other major cities within the UK. This sector provides accommodation for newcomers to the city and those on the first rungs of the property ladder in particular. However, part of this sector remains problematic, with a high level of unfitness. In parts of the city – especially Riverside, Grangetown, Plasnewydd – there are significant numbers homes in multiple occupation, usually offering very poor quality housing. There has also been an expansion of private landlords in areas such as Cathays and Roath to accommodate Cardiff's increasing student population, as well as a growth in 'buy-to-let', especially in central Cardiff and in Cardiff Bay.

The relationship between private home ownership and rented housing mirrors what has happened across the UK over the last 30 years – a decline in the rented sector. In that period, the number of rented homes owned and managed by Cardiff Council fell from 24,600 to little more than 14,300. That is a decline of more than 40 per cent. This was mostly due the transfer of Council-owned homes to owner-occupation under the right-to-buy scheme. Although the Council was the first in the UK to build new Council Houses to rent after 2000. However neither this nor the much more significant growth in housing association provision – especially after 1988 – has offset the loss of Council-owned homes from the rented sector.

Cardiff's vision for housing in the city has broadly remained unchanged since the mid 1970s: seeking to ensure that its residents are able to access good quality, affordable homes. What has changed is the social, economic and policy context in which the Council operates. Moreover, the local housing system itself has changed considerably. Over the last 20 years the Council has placed greater emphasis on working in partnership with a range of statutory, voluntary and private sector organisations, as well as its residents. In addition, in a culture of declining public investment in housing, partnership has been essential to attract additional investment resources. In terms of housing provision, the city remains reliant upon the private sector, and in the social rented sector housing associations have come to play a much greater role, not only as providers but in supporting the improvement of parts of the existing housing stock and promoting neighbourhood regeneration. There has been an emerging and welcome recognition that housing needs to be linked to broader community

and regeneration strategies for Cardiff, as well as policies to deal with crime and disorder, the needs of vulnerable people, health and social care services, and the wider urban environment of Cardiff.

> Happily, Europe is still a Europe of cities, and it will be best and wise to keep it that way as long as possible. One day, they may also explode in size as we have seen elsewhere. It is the great wealth of Europe and the first political task of all Europeans to preserve their cities and remain a civilisation of cities. After love, the city is the most fascinating theme in philosophy, literature and everything, because the city is the most complicated of all.
>
> **BOGDAN BOGDANOVIC**
> THE CITY AND DEMONS (2002)

As the capital city of Wales, Cardiff has traditionally experienced a greater demand for housing than most other parts of the country. This is a function of its size, its population profile and its rate of growth. In addition, it has a wider range of housing needs than other Welsh communities because of the complex mix of its population and the high proportion of demand from single people, as well as its importance as a European capital and a major regional centre of culture and education. However evidence suggests that

housing needs and demands are expanding at a faster rate than the increase in the available housing stock. At present prevailing house prices create severe home ownership problems, particularly for first-time buyers, and the decline of affordable rented provision exacerbates the housing situation.

In the mid 1970s and 1980s the evidence of future requirements for housing tended to be based upon estimates derived from the County Structure Plan, with the anticipated need for publicly-subsidised rented homes based upon numbers registered on the Council's housing register or waiting list. The South Glamorgan Structure Plan approved a housing requirement for Cardiff of 18,700 additional dwellings in the period 1976-1991, or an average of almost 1,250 dwellings per annum. Over time it has been accepted that an increasing share of new provision should be private housing for owner occupation. Cardiff, despite the physical constraints imposed upon it by its physical and administrative boundaries, has met its own needs. In the 1980s this saw the focus of new development on the east of the city around St. Mellons, where private and social rented housing developed side by side. In the more recent period, opportunities for housing development in Cardiff Bay and in the city centre itself, helped to meet the need for additional homes. Now, a new development plan shows a need for a further 16,800 homes in the city over the next decade, with over half to be on previously developed 'brownfield' land. It is anticipated that land will be allocated for 4,000 new homes between Lisvane and Pontprennau, with a further 1,300 homes to be built at St. Mellons.

Over the last 10 years the Council has worked to develop a more detailed picture of housing needs. Research suggests that the extent of the city's housing requirements is much greater than was earlier anticipated. The 2002 Cardiff Housing Needs Survey estimates an annual shortfall of over 2,700 affordable homes. These needs mainly arise from existing households who are involuntarily sharing with others, from new households, from those who are homeless and – to a lesser extent – from new residents who will be moving to the city in future.

Housing needs can also be seen in the numbers of applicants on the Council's housing register, which reached almost 6,200 in April 2004, including more than 1,500 existing tenants seeking transfers, and a growing number of homeless people who are putting pressure on temporary accommodation. Cardiff offered just over

1,100 lettings in 2003-04, compared with almost twice this number in 1986. Housing associations, who now own and manage almost 10,000 properties in Cardiff, are playing their part in meeting housing needs, as are some private landlords. But there is a clear need for additional investment in the provision of new social housing.

The sharp growth of Cardiff in the second half of the 19th Century means a quarter of its homes are more than a hundred years old. From the late 1950s through to the early 1970s, the City Council pursued an active policy of urban renewal, using its powers to acquire and clear areas of sub-standard housing, especially in Butetown. But large swathes of Cardiff are still dominated by streets of Victorian and Edwardian terraced housing. In the mid 1970s the Council shifted the emphasis of its housing renewal policy, taking homes out of planned clearance programmes and electing to encourage their retention and improvement.

The American writer Lewis Mumford once reminded us that 'Human life swings between movement and settlement.' During the last decades an increase of mobility of all kinds is taking place all over the world. People migrate, crossing borders in search of work and a better life. And at regional level, the separation of urban and rural life is disappearing.

MAX VAN DEN BERG
INTERNATIONAL ASSOCIATION
OF PLANNERS

In areas of older private housing, owner-occupiers, private landlords and housing associations have all been encouraged to invest in improving housing conditions. The availability of grant aid, together with an area-based approach to improvement during the 1970s and 1980s, has meant most of the worst physical conditions are

BIG SCREEN HIRE (01242) 676966

The quality of Cardiff's housing is relatively much better than in many other parts of South Wales

gone. In general, the quality of Cardiff's housing is relatively much better than in many other parts of South Wales, and particularly in parts of the South Wales Valleys. Nevertheless, on some issues of housing quality, Cardiff still faces pressing problems of poor housing conditions. These problems are particularly concentrated in certain electoral divisions and sectors of the housing market, especially parts of the private rented sector. Although considerable progress has been made, the changing framework for private housing renewal places additional responsibilities upon the city to develop local responses to the problems of houses that are unfit and in need of repair.

At the turn of the century, almost one in five citizens of Cardiff were pensioners. And where these households may have a range of support needs, often coupled with low or limited incomes, an increasing number in the private sector may be living in poor and unsuitable homes. In the future, a greater emphasis may need to be placed on helping private owners to borrow to maintain and

improve their homes. Using the equity older home owners have could mean they will not have to rely upon financial support from the state for renovation. However, such a shift in emphasis will require not only a change in local policy, but also a re-education of many home owners.

There is also a need to address the problem of housing and environmental quality of the remaining public sector housing stock. A survey undertaken in 2001-02 showed a fifth of Cardiff's houses were built before 1945, and a further third between then and 1964. It is estimated that investment of £112 million is required to meet the Assembly's Welsh Housing Quality Standard by the target date of 2012, with a further £140 million worth of capital investment needed over the next 30 years. Despite this substantial investment requirement, the Council has indicated it does not expect to consider the option of housing stock transfer in relation to Cardiff's remaining Council housing – a process which has already taken place in Bridgend. It may well be, given its past record of investing

both capital and revenue expenditure in its own housing stock, Cardiff has a reasonable prospect of achieving the targets.

In the first decade of the 21st Century there is a growing feeling that Cardiff faces a housing crisis. To deal with that and promote social inclusion and tackle discrimination and disadvantage in communities across the city, the Council confronts a number of challenges. First, the city's population is almost certain to continue to grow. Significantly, changing demographics and household composition suggest the city will require significant additional homes over the next 10-15 years to meet the anticipated increase in households. At the same time, people's expectations about the quality of the environments in which they live, and the level of services they expect, are also set to rise, with the prospect of ever increasing disparities and inequalities across the city.

In recent years demand for home ownership, supported by the ready availability of credit at historically low levels of interest, has moved ahead of supply, fuelling rapid rises in house prices. The future prospects for the Cardiff housing market depend upon the wider economic and political environments. If the local economy continues to grow, and interest rates and unemployment remain relatively low, demand for home ownership across the city is likely to grow even further`. However, owning a home of their own in Cardiff is likely to remain beyond the reach of many people, and if present trends continue, poorer households could be forced out of neighbourhoods which now offer affordable housing. To cope, Cardiff needs strategies not only to preserve a stock of good quality, affordable social

housing, but to increase this provision. At the same time, problems of crime and anti-social behaviour – often centred on small areas – need to be tackled, and the quality of public services improved, not only to ensure that poorer households are not further disadvantaged, but that particular neighbourhoods do not become unpopular places to live.

The social rented homes sector has declined and changed over the last 30 years. The stock of Council housing, in particular, has been very significantly reduced. To some extent housing associations have taken up the slack and become more important providers of affordable, good quality homes. The Council and other social landlords need to continue to make what is a strong case for significantly increased public investment in housing to meet current and future needs. At the same time, the Assembly's setting of a target date of 2012 for housing, to meet the quality standard, will only add to the pressures.

Debate will no doubt continue as to the future ownership and control of social rented housing. The condition of the Council stock is good. The Council's record and reputation as a social landlord is a positive one. And it enjoys the support of its tenants. The city is by no means a monopoly provider of rented homes, meaning it may be able to retain the ownership of its Council housing. However, even if this is the case, there is much for the Council to do in refashioning some of its social housing, engaging more closely with residents and continuing to improve the quality of services. This emphasises the wider strategic role of working with others to ensure needs and demands are fully catered for, and increasingly this may mean politicians looking beyond city boundaries, and working with others within the region to meet housing requirements.

Overall, there remains a need for Cardiff to encourage the provision of additional homes which are well designed and affordable, located in communities which are attractive and sustainable. At the same time, the city needs to work with others to target regeneration investment and activity in some of its less prosperous areas, at the same time ensuring local residents are fully involved in both policy debates and planning processes. Public resources will need to be carefully targeted to meet changing needs, with the Council working closely with others to meet the full range of demands from the city's diverse population, ensuring that its most vulnerable and marginal residents are not excluded from sharing in Cardiff's growing prosperity.

Overall, there remains a need for Cardiff to encourage the provision of additional homes which are well designed and affordable

Viv Jones
Case Manager,
Social Services

" I do the assessments and care planning for vulnerable elderly people in Cardiff, particularly in the Canton area. Since 1993, when the law changed, the emphasis on care has been to avoid institutions, enabling people to remain in their own home with their family where possible.

Of course we could always do with more resources but we have to be realistic and sometimes juggle the services we can provide in order to deal with a particular case.

Society in general is growing older, living longer, putting greater demands on our services. We are constantly looking at new ways to deal with that demand. I've been in this work for 28 years and I wouldn't do anything else. Where else could I be paid to go out every day to help elderly people with their problems? We will all get old – you, me and all my colleagues. That means we will all be on the 'receiving end' of social services eventually. I want to get those services right for the people who need our help now. "

"I've been driving buses for six years. When people, especially men, ask what I do and I say drive a Cardiff Bus, they don't believe it. They see me, five-foot-two, and I can see they're thinking: "She's having me on!" It is not as difficult as you might think, moving a vehicle longer than 30 feet through the streets. But when I was in training, I tried not to look back through the bus. It looked huge!

And then, yes, the next thing they ask is: "Have you pranged this machine?" Only once! It was the weather, believe it or not. There was ice on the road and I bounced off the kerb.

It's a friendly job. You have the chance to help people, especially when you get a nice 'Thank you!' from passengers. A lot of them may be living on their own, a bit isolated. They come out for a few hours and I may be the only one who gives them a cheery hello and a smile. So I can make a big difference.

Every day is different. I don't drive the same route or always work the same shift. I used to work in garden centres. I have qualifications in horticulture but that was getting cut-throat - meeting sales targets, pressurised and all that. I came down to Cardiff Bus on an open day and never left."

Suzanne Chamberlain
Bus Driver,
Cardiff Bus

Tony Smith

Housing

Officer

"Empathy is the 'buzz' word. My role involves working in the community, with people from poorer backgrounds. It's all about being able to understand other people's circumstances. I enjoy the personal touch – and the ability to make decisions that will improve people's lives. You've got to know what you're doing and have your finger 'on the pulse.' For years, I worked with my hands – I even helped build the Butetown Tunnel. My previous experience helps me to relate to people from all backgrounds.

The most difficult part of my job is having to tell a customer: 'No, we haven't got a property for you.' You have to explain to people that while they're way down the waiting list at the moment, they will move up and pretty soon they may get a house.

The Housing team deals with a whole range of issues. Cardiff is a diverse and multi-cultural city – that means working to help people from all kinds of backgrounds. One minute you might be talking to a young mother fleeing domestic violence, the next you might be trying to find accommodation for an asylum seeker.

In this job, you have to be realistic, as well as care about the people you deal with. There is a good support network throughout the Council that helps us to find homes for those in need. If we can't help at this office, we'll work with the Homelessness Section to find a solution. The support system is fantastic. That is what makes the job worthwhile. There aren't many jobs where you have the ability to put a roof over someone's head because they are desperate and in need. It's great to be a part of all that."

Cultural Transformation
Chapter 5

Adapted from text by John Lovering

The city is a partnership of similar persons, for the sake of a life that is the best possible

Aristotle

There has been a real cultural explosion in Cardiff recently. It is a city which has enjoyed a complete make-over over the last few years, and the creative talent, energy and vibe within the city is incredible

Laurence Llewelyn-Bowen, Interior Designer

A city is not just a place where people work. Nor is it just a collection of buildings. A city is a place where people interact with others, work, play, develop friendships and generally give meaning to their lives. What matters most about a city, to those who live in it, is what it feels like to live in. This is a matter of 'culture'. The distinguished Welsh intellectual and novelist Raymond Williams knew Cardiff and the Valleys well. Williams wrote that culture is about the 'structure of feeling' people share.

> No sooner than I'd arrived the other Cardiff had gone, smoke in the memory, these but tinned resemblances, where the boy I was not and the man I am not met, hesitated, left double footsteps, then walked on.
>
> **DANIEL ABSE**
> RETURN TO CARDIFF

Cardiff grew very rapidly from a tiny hamlet to a large city, mainly because it lay astride the supply chain for coal, the fuel for the Royal Navy when it switched from sail to steam ships in the 1840s. The city grew through an influx of immigrants lured by the promise of jobs. They came from all over Wales, elsewhere in the British Isles, and beyond. As the city grew it became home to distinct cultural groups. The Irish formed a quarter of the city's population at one point. But in Cardiff they generally did not polarise into separate communities defined by their religion, as in Liverpool or Glasgow. The Jewish community expanded, especially following outbreaks of anti-Semitism in the Valleys. A conspicuous Italian community also emerged, mainly coming from Emilia Romagna. This diversity gave rise to a vibrant urban culture. The docks area became particularly cosmopolitan, with Wales' first mosque, not far from its first Greek Orthodox Church, next door to a fine Victorian Anglican Church.

Throughout the 20th Century Cardiff fared better than most of the rest of Wales. The Valleys suffered severely from the economic depression of the 1930s. But Cardiff was relatively unscathed, because its economy was by now driven mainly by service and administrative jobs. Guest, Keen and Baldwin helped by transferring their steel works – and its jobs - from Merthyr to East Moors in 1935. Soon afterwards the outbreak of the Second World War brought a mini-boom to the city, and thousands of high-spending US troops. After the war Cardiff generally continued to prosper, although it did not boom as much as many other British cities, and so didn't attract as many new immigrants, especially ethnic minorities from the Commonwealth.

The legacy of this social diversity and relative economic stability left Cardiff with a rich store of places, organisations, and talents, for cultural activities of all sorts. These were visible in the form of a

Better known outside Cardiff were Shirley Bassey and Iris Williams who had cut their teeth in the local music scene and gone on to be major British stars

large number of churches and chapels, for example, and also a number of impressive music halls, pubs and clubs. The New Theatre had opened in 1906, joining the Empire, the Grand Theatre in Westgate Street, the Prince of Wales, the Theatre Royal and the Philharmonic in St Mary Street. Only the New Theatre remains as a theatre, while the others have either been demolished or converted into pubs.

Post-industrial societies spend a lot of time trying to commemorate the past: to give status and pride to something that society, at another level, has seemed to cast aside. Loss of community memory is terrible. But we need to go beyond commemoration and nostalgia... We must remember to remember but also remember to dream, and one role of the arts and artists is to enlarge our capacity to dream, to foster the imagination where it exists and rekindle it where it has died.

GERAINT TALFAN DAVIES
CHAIRMAN, THE ARTS COUNCIL OF WALES

The Victorian legacy still shapes Cardiff's cultural character. There were plenty of venues where people could meet, drink and entertain each other in various ways. In terms of music, Cardiff in the '60s and '70s had a reputation for R'n'B and jazz, drawing especially on local musicians, both black and white. By contrast the

Valleys were better known for rock bands such as Man and Budgie, whose influence lived on to the 2000s via the Manic Street Preachers and the Stereophonics. Cardiff was more like Liverpool or Bristol, where a distinctive local musical tradition grew out of the presence of large numbers of black Americans during the War many of whom were stationed at what is now the Heath Hospital. Transatlantic links continued afterwards, most famously symbolised by Paul Robeson. He had relatives in Butetown but was also widely admired in the Valleys for his support of oppressed peoples, and affection for mining communities.

The outlook has always been bright for Cardiff. It's long been a city of craftsmen, artists and learning and is a powerhouse of culture driving forward the whole of Wales. With the exceptional talent under its skies, I can see the city going on to scale even greater heights!

SIAN LLOYD
TV PERSONALITY

Thanks to such connections, American and West Indian music came to Cardiff long before it was played on British radio or TV stations. Photographs from the 1960s show listeners giving rapt attention to Vince Parker, a Caribbean born musician who played in Butetown pubs. Better known outside Cardiff were Shirley Bassey and Iris Williams who had cut their teeth in the local music scene and went on to become major British stars. North of the old 'divide' marked by the Swansea to London railway line, the Hennessys became one of the few nationally-known acts to draw explicitly on their Cardiff background. Into the 1980s pubs such as the Royal Oak in Splott were home to a dynamic R&B and rock scene, nurturing performers who went on to become national and

international figures. The most successful in 'chart' terms were rock guitarist and record producer Dave Edmunds, and Terry Williams of Dire Straits, though neither were Cardiff born. Bands like Young Marble Giants, the Darling Buds and a few others enjoyed their 15-minutes of fame in the 1980s, followed 20 years later by Hear'say's Noel Sullivan, born in Cardiff. But Cardiff has not produced any major pop acts, even in the late 1990s heyday of 'Cool Cymru'. It has been better known in the musical world as the home of the Welsh National Opera (WNO).

By the 1990s many of the old Victorian venues had disappeared due to redevelopment, along with the live music scene rooted in them. The do-it-yourself music and arts culture based in local clubs and pubs was replaced by a better organised, larger-scale, and more commercial popular music culture, as in most other British and American cities. Some small live music venues have hung on, and some new ones emerged, such as Chapter, Barfly, and the Toucan Club, providing outlets for live music. But there are many more clubs dedicated to recorded music and DJs. Best known are some

stunning new large-scale buildings dedicated to the arts - and to sport. Thanks to these the character, and the setting, of local culture has been transformed.

The last decade and a half has seen a growing emphasis on, and confidence in, Welsh identity, and this has given Cardiff a new cultural significance, both at the level of street culture and in more formal arts scenes. But Cardiff's culture is mainly shaped by influences common to all British cities, rooted in suburbanisation, the growth of consumerism, the general liberalisation of British lifestyles and the growth of large-scale corporations in the arts and cultural industries. Cardiff is a culturally lively place, but its culture is somewhat less distinctive than in the past. This has opened up a wide range of new entertainment opportunities for all, but it has also caused some to worry about the direction of change.

Cardiff grew as a city on the basis of large-scale manual labour. But the docks declined in the inter-war decades, never again to be a major employer. The railways too ceased to be a major source of

Cardiff is a culturally lively place, but its culture is somewhat less distinctive than in the past.

jobs in the 1950s, and the East Moors Steelworks ran down from the 1960s, finally closing in 1978. Cardiff was and remains a predominantly working class city, but the character of the working class, and its cultural life, changed radically. From the 1970s all the growth was in non-manual work, especially in retail and offices, and especially amongst women. By the 1990s the employment structure of the city was much like that of any medium-sized British or European city. Shopping, catering, hotels, and the public-sector-dominated categories of administration, health and education now account for over half of employment, and two-thirds amongst women.

Although it is still widely used amongst older people, the traditional language of class began to seem outdated. And the divide between high-art and popular culture began to dissolve. The local authorities speeded-up the re-imaging of Cardiff by changing the names of some of the most stoutly working class areas - Tiger Bay and Rat Island officially disappeared. More and more people saw themselves as middle-class or as professionals, especially those employed in the civil service and other government-funded areas such as the University and the media, and the self-employed. First Minister Rhodri Morgan has described Cardiff as a city of 'two cultures', one rooted in the local working class and the other in the often incoming

'governing' middle class – respectively ' the industrial and the satsuma way of life'.

> There has been a real cultural explosion in Cardiff recently. It is a city which has enjoyed a complete make-over over the last few years, and the creative talent, energy and vibe within the city is incredible.
>
> **LAURENCE LLEWELYN-BOWEN**
> INTERIOR DESIGNER

The growth of consumerism especially from the 1970s, had a huge physical and cultural influence on cities, and Cardiff is a textbook example. From St David's Centre to Culverhouse Cross to Cardiff Gate to St David's 2 – and the proposed new stadium for a complex at Leckwith incorporating new athletics and football stadia, 40,000 square metres of retailing and a range of community benefits. And this in turn influenced other more obviously cultural changes. The opening of the St Davids Centre in 1981 for example, was a landmark in the development of a new consumer culture. It was followed a year later by the opening of St Davids Hall. Part-funded by a £4m donation from the Heron Corporation, this was Cardiff's first world-class music venue and put the city on the circuit for major UK and international touring acts, especially in

The growth of consumerism especially from the 1970's had a huge physical and cultural influence on cities, and Cardiff is a textbook example

classical and light pop music. In 1993 the Queen opened the Cardiff International Arena, seating 5,000, an even bigger leap in the city's ability to attract national and international artists, and the conference trade.

In 1997 the UCI cinema complex opened in the Atlantic Wharf Leisure Village, targeting the family market and car users from Bridgend to the Severn Bridge. Soon afterwards two more multiplexes opened in the city centre, this time aiming to attract more students and young people. Like most cities Cardiff lost its traditional locally-owned cinemas. A Bollywood cinema in Roath in the early 2000s did not survive. Chapter Arts Centre alone remains to provide more 'art house' movies.

The reinvention of the local theatre scene can be traced to the cultural upheavals of the 1960s. The British government was committed to subsidising the arts, and in 1967 the Arts Council of Wales was spun out of the Arts Council of Great Britain. It immediately became involved in a vast range of activities throughout Wales, many in Cardiff.

At around the same time a different and less top-down sort of cultural energy was emerging from the diverse movements that made up the 60s. Chapter Arts Centre is the legacy, beginning as a typical arts centre of the time. Its first major event was a six-hour open-air Pink Floyd concert in Sophia Gardens. In 1971 it settled in the disused Canton High School. With funding from the Arts Council, the local authority, Sgrin, and Europa Cinemas, Chapter became a core cultural institution in Cardiff. It now attracts around 250,000 users a year, even although its location is far from ideal – being a long way from the bustle of the city centre. Chapter hoped to open a waterside facility in the regenerated Cardiff Bay but was unable to secure funding.

Culture is now Cardiff's core business and its breathtaking pace of change over the past decade is set to continue well into the new century.

CARDIFF 2008 CITY OF CULTURE BID

In 1973 the Sherman Theatre, funded by the Sherman family and Cardiff University, opened in Senghennydd Road next to the new student union. In the 1990s it established a relationship with the Manic Street Preachers. In 1987 the relocated Norwegian Church opened as a small gallery and performance venue. For 30 years Chapter, the Sherman, and the New Theatre have provided Cardiff with a wide variety of stage entertainment, and have nurtured state management, acting, cinema, and other skills. In

Much of the distinctive cultural strength of Wales derives from vigorous tradition of community arts

the new century they have been joined by a striking new partner, on a much larger scale, in the form of the Wales Millennium Centre (WMC) in Cardiff Bay.

The Arts Council inherited well-equipped theatres, specifically in Bangor and Cardiff. Plans to build an entirely new theatre however had to wait until the 1980s, when another organisation became involved and triggered the necessary changes in planning and widening of funding opportunities. The Cardiff Bay Development Corporation was set up in April 1987 to apply locally the Thatcher Government's strategy of regenerating run-down areas by attracting property investment. The Corporation eventually succeeded in turning the waterfront into an area in which developers, the construction industry, Associated British Ports (the landowner) as well as companies seeking office space and political parties found a common purpose. The Corporation's aim was "To put Cardiff on the international map as a superlative maritime city which will stand comparison with any such city in the world, thereby enhancing the image and economic well-being of Cardiff and Wales as a whole". And in accordance with new thinking about economic development, cultural projects were given priority from the start.

These ambitions first crystallised around the project to develop a new home for the WNO. The story of the WMC began with a 1994 competition to design a new opera house. The design by Zaha Hadid, the acclaimed Iranian-American architect, was however finally deemed too exotic. Britain's Percy Thomas was commissioned to produce an alternative design that would be both "unmistakably Welsh and internationally outstanding". The result was the 1,800 seat WMC, which opened in November 2004 at a cost of £104 million money provided by public and private funding, including one private overseas donation of £20 million. This has provided a new home for several organisations including the WNO, Urdd Gobaith Cymru and Diversions Dance Company. The external appearance of the building is controversial – it has been renamed by some locals as the 'Armadillo' – but the management strategy aims to use the state-of-the-art facilities which lie within it to promote a wide range of cultural activities,

The emergence of 'clubland' in the city centre, and now the Bay, has been a major feature of cultural change in Cardiff in the period of its regeneration

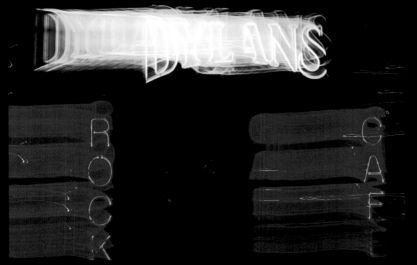

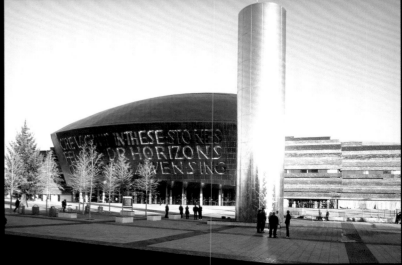

exemplifying the new crossovers between popular and high-art. It hopes to attract an audience of nearly two million a year.

Much of the distinctive cultural strength of Wales derives from a vigorous tradition of community arts. Although the WNO is now a major international player, it grew out of a local choral society tradition. Wales also has its own national dance company - Diversions, which was created in 1983 by Roy Campbell-Moore and Ann Sholem. The company commissions and premiers work by international choreographers and also delivers workshops to schools and colleges.

Community arts groups and related activities have played an important role in Cardiff and the hope is that this will grow. The Sherman Theatre has engaged local people, especially young people, in a range of productions that have been significant locally and culturally, although they have not had the same impact on Cardiff's external image as events such as the Rugby World Cup or buildings such as the WMC. The MAS Festival in the Bay is also thriving, celebrating cultural diversity in one of its historic locations. This is also reflected in guerrilla radio. The new WMC is committed to building on this tradition, and offers a superb new platform for local creativity.

The growth of popular culture from the 1960s has given rise to a whole new set of cultural industries and changing lifestyles. Dancing is now the number one cultural activity of the British, a quarter of all households participating at least once a year - more than play sport. The emergence of 'clubland' in the city centre, and now the Bay, has been a major feature of cultural change in Cardiff in the period of its regeneration.

In the 1990s many locally-owned establishments were taken over by UK-national chain pubs, clubs and venues. The driving force was the Beer Orders of 1989, and related changes in the licensing guidelines followed by magistrates, which had the effect of shifting the emphasis from controlling alcohol consumption to maximising

competition. These triggered a revolution in British drinking patterns and city nightlife, which have had a massive impact on Cardiff. Long-established Irish pubs gave way to 'branded' Irish pubs. A set of sports bars replaced old pubs in and around St Mary Street. Springbok Bars are part of the Old Monk Group, with 76 outlets. Bar Oz is part of a UK-wide chain, while Walkabout Inns, along with Bar Risa and Jongleurs is owned by Regent Inns plc. Jumping Jacks, Life, and the Hard Rock Café are all owned by Luminar Leisure, the largest nightclub operator in the UK with 300 outlets and over 15 per cent of all clubs. Together with bars such as Flares, Ha-Has and Cuba, the city centre is an evening magnet for local people, students and visitors.

The growth of Cardiff's clubland in the 1990 has engaged more people more directly than any other aspect of cultural change, as dramatised in the movie 'Human Traffic' Cardiff's flowering of bars and clubs, reaching a capacity in the early 2000s of around 70,000, made it the partying capital of South Wales, and according to some, of Britain.

This revolution was driven by a combination of market forces and policy. Since the early 1990s cultural policy has risen to the top of the agenda for many local authorities. Unlike manufacturing, cultural development, especially when associated with physical development such as new buildings, is a field in which local authorities can have a significant influence – especially if they work in partnership with private investors.

The Cardiff Bay Development Corporation played a critical role in setting the new model, passing it on to Cardiff Council. In 1993 the Council's forerunner had adopted the view that cultural strategies offered the greatest potential for raising the perceived competitiveness of the city. Cardiff's own population growth was never going to lift it to the scale associated with a major European city - but by making itself more meaningful as the 'capital of the Valleys', Cardiff could count itself as commanding a population nearer a million than 300,000. Making Cardiff more central culturally thereby became a key objective in the economic competitiveness strategy. To this end the Council began to encourage a European-style café culture. The first manifestation of this was the regeneration of Mill Lane, site of the former Glamorgan Canal. The regeneration of the nearby Brewery Quarter was completed in 2004.

The increasing tendency of planning authorities to impose public art obligations on developers can often be viewed as a vexing obstacle containing potential risk. However, with good management a very positive result can be achieved.

T.B.DUFFY
MEPC LTD COMMERCIAL PROPERTY DEVELOPERS

The Summer Festival to Winter Wonderland and the Calennig celebrations have been successful in boosting the image of Cardiff, and attracted visitors

The UK Government's decision to host the 1998 European Summit in Cardiff gave a huge boost to the city's international image. Showing the city could successfully and peacefully manage an important international event demonstrated that Cardiff was capable of acting like a European capital.

Cardiff Council also took on the Corporation's strategy of promoting pop and classical concerts in the Bay's Oval Basin, and a range of activities, from the Summer Festival to Winter Wonderland and the Calennig celebrations have been successful in boosting the image of Cardiff, and attracted visitors. As the new century approached, the role of cultural projects in the regeneration of the city leaped to a new level, thanks to new opportunities arising in sport.

The bid by Cardiff to become UK candidate for the European City of Culture in 2008 consolidated links between various authorities and arts organisations, especially the Council and the Welsh Assembly Government, which set up a company – Cardiff 2008 – to spearhead the bid.

Take me somewhere good
CARDIFF 2008 CITY OF CULTURE BID

When the European City of Culture programme began in 1985 it was seen as a chance for a renewed focus by cities on their cultural heritage and their distinctive cultural identity and vitality. The selection process is a competition, the winners being the city considered most able to represent their country and Europe by putting on a year long celebration of international cultural events highlighting European culture.

The UK was allocated 2008 as the year in which one of its cities would be chosen and Cardiff was one of 12 UK cities that entered the competition to become European Capital of Culture in 2008. Cardiff made the short list of six cities that was announced in October and narrowly missed out to Liverpool in the final round of judging. As a result of its bid Cardiff was awarded a mark of excellence recognising its cultural wealth and designating the city as a "Centre of Culture".

> Cardiff has been given a tremendous impetus to artistic and cultural activity in the city and we must now build on this. Cardiff celebrates 50 years as our capital city in 2005 and much of the work which was put into the bid will contribute to making that a celebration of which all Wales can be proud; and which will provide another major boost to the Welsh tourism industry.
>
> **PETER HAIN**
> SECRETARY OF STATE FOR WALES (2002-)

It was hoped that a successful bid for Cardiff would shift European focus to the city and Wales for a whole year, celebrating the unique contribution we make to the culture of Europe with 12 packed months of world class events throughout Cardiff and Wales. The bid recognised that Cardiff is Europe's youngest capital, a

multicultural city which serves a country rich in both traditional and contemporary culture. Cardiff's bid highlighted the new ways that the city can work for the people and the cultural communities across the whole of Wales and recognised that sense of place is a defining quality of Welsh culture.

We invested in Cardiff for a reason: it's going places. Cardiff has a thriving arts and cultural scene, with a network of facilities and events. As one of the coolest hotels of the world, we are delighted to contribute to the success of this retro city.

JOHN MALKOVICH
HOLLYWOOD ACTOR AND CO-OWNER OF THE BIG SLEEP HOTEL

Sport has always been a vital element of popular culture and Cardiff reflected this. It has long been a centre for rugby in the form of the former National Stadium, for cricket with Sophia Gardens becoming Glamorgan Cricket Club's headquarters in 1985, and for football at Cardiff City Football Club's ground at Ninian Park. In 1986 ice-skating was added in the form of the Cardiff Devils. In the 1990s the audience for events in Cardiff sports facilities became much more international.

In 1995 the Welsh Rugby Union proposed building a new stadium in a bid to host the 1999 Rugby World Cup. With the active support and cooperation of South Glamorgan County Council, the £130 million 72,500 Millennium Stadium was built funded with a National Lottery contribution of £40 million. The Rugby World

Cup was a huge success, enabling the stadium to follow up by attracting the FA Cup and other major football finals, displaced from London due to the rebuilding of Wembley Stadium. Unlike many cities, Cardiff's magnificent new stadium is right in the heart of town. On match days the excitement echoes throughout the city's shopping centre. It is also a superb facility for major pop and rock concerts, motorsport and corporate events. In a bid to diversify its range of uses further the stadium has introduced a new screen which reduces its effective size, making it more viable for large but not gigantic pop acts. Cardiff's move into the international sports event markets gathered pace with a successful bid to host the British leg of the FIA World Rally Championship.

My first great success was in the 100m representing Wales in the Junior National Games - so it's great to have seen Cardiff discovering itself as a centre of Welsh sporting excellence. With the Millennium Stadium, Cardiff has proved itself capable of hosting world class sporting events. It's a city of possibility - a training ground for the next generation of sportsmen and women. It feels very rich in involvement, participation and support.

TANNI GREY-THOMSON
ATHLETE

As the Millennium Stadium was being built, Cardiff City Football Club put forward proposals to replace its Ninian Park ground with a new 60,000-seat stadium at Leckwith providing an academy status football facility. Cardiff Council, the land owner, would grant a 125-year lease for a peppercorn rent for the football stadium site and new retail and housing developments would largely pay for the new football and athletics facilities. One of many conditions of the lease requires the Club to implement an anti-hooliganism policy.

Together with the National Indoor Athletics Centre, opened at the University of Wales Institute Cardiff's Cyncoed campus in January 2000, these amount to a stunning new cluster of world class sports facilities. Plans are also being developed for a national academy of sport in Cardiff – drawing on the work of the Sports Council of Wales, Elite Cymru, the Welsh Rugby Union, Glamorgan County Cricket Club, Cardiff City Football Club and Disability Sport Wales.

Reflect on what could be the fundamental similarities of cultural buildings: are they not all basically to do with regeneration? Are they not all intended to attract commercial investment? Do they not all depend, ultimately, on hitting visitor targets regardless of any other merit they possess?

JONATHAN ADAMS
ARCHITECTS WITHOUT ARCHITECTURE IN
TOUCHSTONES

The need to provide a replacement for Cardiff Empire Pool, demolished in the late 1990s to make way for the Millennium Stadium, triggered one of the most dramatic new sports developments currently underway - the International Sports Village. This £700 million project is being built on reclaimed land in Cardiff Bay and is intended to include state-of-the-art sports, leisure and entertainment facilities including residences, hotels, bars, restaurants and retail outlets. The Village will be centred on a new multi-use swimming pool, an 4,000 seat multi-use arena, a snow dox, a casino and conference centre. The development, which will take seven years to complete, got underway in September 2003. Twice as large financially as St David's 2, this is the most ambitious development yet planned for Cardiff.

Cardiff has attracted corporations seeking to invest in the 'play economy' of pubs, clubs and eating places mainly because it is a large city – larger, in effect, than its own population base thanks to its regional role for the Valleys and surrounding areas.

But other culture-related changes in Cardiff since the 1970s have been linked to the fact that it is Wales' capital city. This drew the major cultural industries to the city, beginning with BBC Wales in 1967 followed by HTV in the 1970s and S4C in 1984.

The steady expansion of the University since the 1960s, and the College of Music and Drama, subsequently gave a further boost to the city's cultural production capacity. Cardiff College of Education became the South Glamorgan Institute of Higher education in 1976, later becoming UWIST, which merged with the University College in the late 1980s. The University College Hospital of Wales opened at the Heath in 1971, and merged with Cardiff University in 2004. The predominance of higher education institutions enables Cardiff to produce a relatively high output of scientific publications, helping it to score highly on indicators of the 'Knowledge Economy'. But these institutions make their biggest economic and cultural contribution through the employment they provide, and the market created by the spending of tens of thousands of students.

Cardiff has attracted corporations seeking to invest in the 'play economy' of pubs, clubs and eating places

The steady expansion of the University since the 1960's, and the College of Music and Drama subsequently gave a further boost to the city's cultural production capacity

Cardiff is a leading example of a city which grew as a Victorian centre of trade and has since transformed into a centre of consumption, not least of entertainment, especially by young people. With around 30,000 students, further and higher education provides a huge stimulus to the demand and talent, required by entertainment and other cultural activities. The steady growth of the 'Youth Economy' has been extended with the growth of visitors to the city for evening entertainment, as Cardiff's role as a regional centre has expanded. It has had a profound impact on the economic and cultural development of the city.

> Entertainment, adventure and experience are added to passive and active recreation. Beside the use of place, individuals want to undergo a sense of place. Pleasure is bought, the free-time industry flourishes. In addition to traditional provisions for open space this consumerism demands extensive use of land and new designs.
>
> **MAX VAN DEN BERG**
> INTERNATIONAL SOCIETY OF CITY AND REGIONAL PLANNERS

High-profile cultural developments became economically desirable in the 1990s because they were seen as a way of raising image and competitiveness. In the 2000s another economic aspect of culture has attracted policy makers. Cultural policies are now recognised as important in shaping social diversity, and diversity is good for innovation and competitiveness. The strategy to develop a European style evening culture, alongside the growth of clubland, has gathered momentum. It is increasingly seen as the best way to encourage the development of a new population profile and new enterprise culture which will boost the city's long-term ability to innovate and develop an economy able to compete in global markets.

One aspect of social diversity which has had a prominent impact on cultural planning strategies in many cities in the US and Europe is the presence of a gay culture. The growth of the 'Gay Villages' of San Francisco or Manchester, for example, are seen as demonstrating how social diversity can also bring commercial and wider benefits. This is one influence leading to the growth of official respect – and planning – for this aspect of diversity in Cardiff, not previously known as an outstandingly gay-friendly city. The Council

supports the annual Mardi Gras - organised by Safer Cardiff Ltd., a charity committed to combating homophobic hate crime. Over 35,000 people attended the 2003 event. At a more everyday level, planning has nurtured the growth of a gay 'quarter' between Mill Lane and Charles Street.

Over the past three decades Cardiff has gained a set of striking new buildings dedicated to the arts and sport. At the same time it has seen the growth of a range of commercially successful independent arts enterprises such as the Bay Gallery and Tactile Bosch. The evening life of the city has beyond recognition by the growth of bars, eating places, and 'clubland'. Together these have transformed both the cultural character of Cardiff and its physical appearance.

One effect has been to reunite Cardiff with the Valleys. Early in the last century the city was linked to the hinterland by flows of coal. Now the flows are of people. Cardiff's labour market depends on tens of thousands of daily commuters from the Valleys. Tens of thousands also come to enjoy the 'play economy'. Shopping, formal culture, sport, nightlife and days out at the Bay bring the Valleys into

Cardiff more than ever before. And for major events people travel in from all over Wales, England and beyond. Cardiff has indeed become Wales's cultural capital. But the speed of recent success brings new challenges.

Cardiff is host to a large number of artists, producers and performers in a range of fields, from ceramics to film-making to DJ's. Like any capital city, it attracts more than its share of performers and cultural entrepreneurs. But Cardiff will need to find ways to nurture and retain cultural players of all sorts if it is not to be left behind as they build their careers by moving up to a bigger – national and international - league. For example, three-quarters of the UK's professional musicians live in London. Devolution has not yet altered the fact that Wales' most famous stars live in England or California.

It is widely recognised, not least by the Welsh Assembly, that new kinds of strategies are needed to promote training and career development. They will require new kinds of co-operation between the Council, educators, entrepreneurs and artists.

Projects to link these players, and the new facilities, with the network of community arts and local sports groups could play a major role here.

This is the 'human capital' dimension of the problem of sustainability. Another dimension concerns the 'physical capital'. As cultural developments have become more closely geared to property-investment projects, they have become more dependent on investor expectations. But these are subject to forces beyond Cardiff's influence. Recent successes have been made possible by circumstances that may not last indefinitely. Global property markets are, some believe, set for a period of instability. Other cities in the UK and Europe are energetically seeking to compete in the sports and gambling markets. The worst scenario is a change in investor perceptions causes difficulties in completing a major project, leading to underused capacity. This deters further investment, something that has regularly happened in the office market. A downturn in the flow of investment would increase the pressure to concentrate on immediate money-earning projects such as casinos , and could damage the wider strategy for diversity and a 'European-style'. If the Sports Village became instead a Gambling Village, this could have major cultural as well as economic implications.

Cultural transformation has been possibly the central component of Cardiff's regeneration. But it is double-edged. The ghost of Raymond Williams might wonder about the 'structure of feeling' associated with the new commercial and official culture. It has brought wonderful new facilities. Yet the city is in many ways culturally less distinctive, less 'different' than it ever was. The same branded clubs, bars, bookshops, cinemas, and many of the same performers, can be found in many other cities. Some worry that Cardiff is losing its distinctiveness: 'There should be more emphasis on real Welsh culture – music, cooking, and history'. Some older people feel uncomfortable in the city centre in the evening.

The booming 'play economy' seen along St Mary Street on a Friday night represents a major economic and cultural success for Cardiff. It has been largely independent of the subsidised growth of high-profile large-scale sports and arts complexes but it does not clearly connect with the cultural strategy for competitiveness, nor with the wish to promote the arts and culture. This may lead to some tension. The effects of concentrating large numbers of people around alcohol consumption are not necessarily conducive to the kind of cultural development that policy makers seek. Binge drinking, drug misuse and consequent street violence are common and costly. They are however, deeply embedded in popular habits, and it should not be assumed, as it sometimes is, that they are much worse than in the past. But they do not fit well into the picture of a Cardiff which is evolving: a European-style evening culture, a civilised environment in which all feel comfortable.

So for both economic and quality of life reasons it seems timely to reappraise recent developments. Are they sustainable? Do they fit the kind of cultural development that is desirable? Since the years of the Cardiff Bay Development Corporation the key policy assumption has been that cultural investments are important

Cultural transformation has been possibly the central component of Cardiff's regeneration

because they can make Cardiff a more attractive place to live and work and so boost its competitiveness. But the real benefits of major developments will need to be identified more precisely, especially if they seem to demand ever larger and potentially more risky projects. And the goal of competitiveness needs to be balanced against other reasons for 'planning for culture' – such as the arguments that this can directly improve the quality of life, and that it can create new ways for people to participate together.

A proper balance will have been found when the new physical infrastructure becomes a set of spaces for new social interactions and uplifting activities and experiences. Culture, from opera to skateboarding, requires not only appropriate physical settings. If it is to be both economically viable and socially valuable, it needs a social infrastructure as well. The strategy needs to embrace 'soft infrastructures' as well as property and events. Building this will be the number one challenge for the next decade.

"

Cardiff was a flagship Council for sport and leisure in the 70s and 80s, and we were the envy of other local authorities. Now, in addition to the Council's efforts, there is a boom in private, commercial facilities as well. The emphasis on sport is huge in this city – the new International Sport Village in the Bay is an example. There's been huge growth in sports provision in schools. We've got 400 sports clubs in Cardiff.

Sport can deal with a lot of challenges for young people and help to tackle crime and delinquency, exclusion and health. Often sport in school can mean a big difference in truancy, and also give us a chance to interact with parents, to engage with them in depth. And it doesn't stop there. We have specific schemes to deal with drugs and alcohol abuse with youth programmes beyond the school day.

I played hockey and tennis, and after college worked the sport and leisure business for 20 years. This job gives me the chance to push for sport development, to grow sport with a team that is now the largest of any Welsh local authority, and the fourth largest in the UK.

I have no doubt we are actually making an impact, changing the lives of young people, improving their health. Cardiff has produced some fantastic athletes. On the playing fields of our schools, I'm sure there are more we'll hear about in future.

"

Stephen Morris
Sport Cardiff
Manager

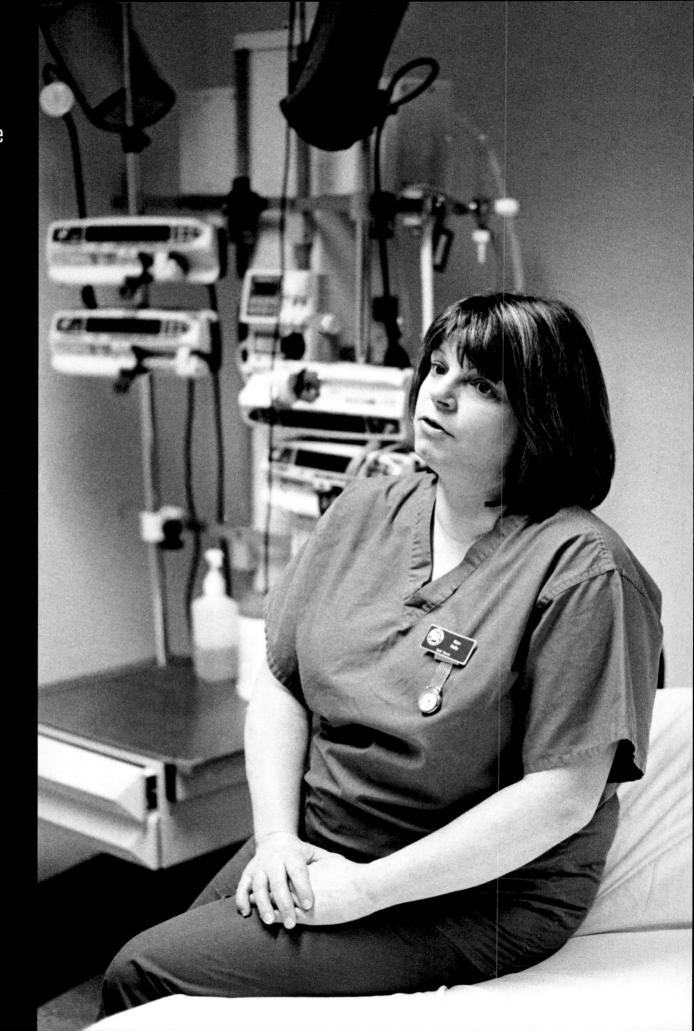

Sian Kelly
Intensive Care
Staff Nurse,
Llandough
Hospital

"I've got a wonderful manager. This job is flexible and I can work flexibly to suit being with my two children. In intensive care, you get patients here who are very sick. Seeing them getting better and moving them back down to a ward after being in the high dependency unit, that's fulfilling. Even if we know they are not going to get better, it's making sure they have a peaceful end. I'm there with them and their family so that everything that can be done is done.

I've been doing this for three years since I finished working on the wards. Some of the patients who were very ill sometimes come back to thank us. And when they look healthy and happy, it's nice beyond words.

The public generally only see ward nurses, and they are stressed and stretched. Any young person who wants to enter nursing today should specialise as I had a chance to do."

"

My grandparents came from Ireland and settled in the Splott area of Cardiff. Two of their sons were police officers. It's a bit of a family tradition. People from my family have been continuously serving as police officers in Cardiff since the 1940s. There are five of us in policing at the moment. It's in our genes. I've got a brother who is a Superintendent here. Another brother is in the National Crime Squad. A cousin serves over in Barry, and another has just retired from policing and is now working for Cardiff Council.

This is a diverse job. I come to work and really don't know what I'll face that day. Policing is also more specialised now. You can do a number of jobs – criminal investigation, traffic – there are so many different areas.

The British police serve the Queen. We swear allegiance to Her Majesty and not the government of the day. We're a Crown organisation steeped in history. And above all, we police by consent of the public. All these things, plus the fact we don't routinely bear arms, makes the British police almost unique in the world.

Our work would be even more effective if we could get a bit more public engagement. It may sound a bit old fashioned but it's about talking to your neighbours, knowing those who live next door, taking an interest in the people along your street, taking some pride in your neighbourhood, getting engaged and involved – looking out for each other. I and every other policeman would like to see a lot more of that.

"

PICTURE CREDITS

Front Cover	Millennium Stadium and Taff Riverwalk	David Hurn
Front Cover	Last Night of the Proms 2004, St Davids Hall	David Hurn
Contents	Last Night of the Proms 2004, St Davids Hall	David Hurn
Contents	Principal dancer for St Petersburg Ballet in Swan Lake, St Davids Hall	David Hurn
Contents	Last Night of the Proms 2004, St Davids Hall	David Hurn
6	Dame Shirley Bassey	Cardiff Council
7	Cardiff Bay Inner Harbour	Ffotograff
9	Wales Grand Slam Winners	Getty Images
10	Millennium Stadium from Wood Street bridge	Ffotograff
12	A walk with Grandfather in Roath, 1973	David Hurn
13	Millennium Stadium tour	David Hurn
13	Football fans in Cardiff for FA Cup Final 2004	David Hurn
14	Playtime at Mount Stuart Primary School, Butetown	David Hurn
16	Sculpture 'People Like Us' and tribute to Diana Princess of Wales, 1997	David Hurn
17	Coal Wagons in Cardiff Docks	Cardiff Council
18	Pierhead Building, Cardiff Bay	Cardiff Council
18	Coal Mine	Ffotograff
18	Coal Miners	Ffotograff
19	Coal Washing	Getty Images
19	Coal Miners	Cardiff Council
20	Graduation Day at Cardiff University, 1978	David Hurn
21	Soccer in the shadow of East Moors Steelworks, 1978	David Hurn
22	Street Artist performing on Queen Street	David Hurn
23	Cardiff Bay Inner Harbour pre-Barrage	David Hurn
23	Cardiff County Hall by night	Cardiff Council
23	Converted warehouses in Atlantic Wharf	Cardiff Council
23	Atlantic Wharf Leisure Village	Cardiff Council
24	Crowds celebrate Wales' try against South Africa, 2004	David Hurn
26	NCM Building, Cardiff Bay	Cardiff Council
27	Graduation Day at Cardiff University, 1978	David Hurn
28	Butetown Link Road	Cardiff Council
28	Butetown Link Road	Cardiff Council
28	Butetown Link Road	Cardiff Council
28	Concorde at Cardiff International Airport	Cardiff Council
28	Derelict Dock in Cardiff Bay	Ffotograff
30	Street Performers on Queen Street, Summer Festival 2004	David Hurn
31	Cardiff Docks	Ffotograff
33	MAS Carnival procession in Mermaid Quay, 2004	David Hurn
33	Interactive exhibit at Techniquest, Cardiff Bay	Ffotograff
33	Cardiff Bay Visitor Centre	Cardiff Council
33	New business in Cardiff Bay	Cardiff Council
34	Victory Podium, Wales GB Rally 2004	David Hurn
35	Rehearsal for the Welsh National Opera, 2002	David Hurn
35	New business in Cardiff Bay	Cardiff Council
36	BBC Wales Headquarters, National Assembly Building, Cardiff Bay	Cardiff Penknife Ltd
36	Cardiff Bay	Cardiff Council
36	Press Room at the Tsunami Concert, 2005	David Hurn
37	Driver signing autographs, Wales GB Rally 2005	David Hurn
38	Wales v New Zealand, 2004	David Hurn
39	Miners Strike March	David Hurn
40	Gareth Edwards Scores at the National Stadium, 1976	David Hurn
41	Cardiff City lose 3-1 to Chelsea at Ninian Park, 1977	David Hurn
42	'Navigation & Mining' Statue in Cathays Park, Cardiff	Ffotograff
43	Poetry Recital in the foyer of the Wales Millennium Centre	David Hurn
44	Playtime at Mount Stuart Primary School, Butetown	David Hurn
46	Sian Love, Welsh Teacher Corpus Christi High School	David Hurn
49	Tony Burnell, C2C Customer Service Representative	David Hurn
50	Summer relaxation in Cardiff Bay	David Hurn
51	Anti racism rally in Cardiff, 1978	David Hurn
52	Summer in Cardiff Bay	David Hurn
52	View south down River Taff	Ffotograff
53	View south over Pontcanna	Ffotograff
54	Cardiff Food and Drink Festival, Cardiff Bay	Ffotograff
56	Playtime at Mount Stuart Primary School, Butetown	David Hurn
57	View north over Cardiff	Ffotograff
59	Aerial view towards city centre	Cardiff Council

CREDITS

Cardiff Council thanks its staff and
Cardiff University for their contribution
towards this unique book. Special thanks
are due also to:

Don Barr
Dame Shirley Bassey
Peter Cope
Marc Davies
David Hurn
Richard Jones
Frank Moloney
Ewart Parkinson

Phil Boland
Gillian Bristow
Richard Cowell
Bella Dicks
Andrew Flynn
Alex Franklin
Neil Harris
Alan Hooper
John Lovering
Brian Morgan
Kevin Morgan
Jane Mudd
John Punter
Bon Smith
Chris Yewlett
Mike Ungersma

Tony Burnell
Sue Chamberlain
Mike Edmonds
Lynda Griffiths
Viv Jones
Sian Kelly
Sian Love
Annie Middleton
Steve Morris
Rob Murphy
Tony Smith
Ian Tumelty